THE JOY OF CREATION

the story of

Clara Schumann

THE JOY OF CREATION

the story of
Clara Schumann

MORGAN REYNOLDS
PUBLISHING

Greensboro, North Carolina

Classical Composers
series

Johann Sebastian Bach

Johannes Brahms

George Frideric Handel

Fanny Mendelssohn

Clara Schumann

Giuseppe Verdi

Antonio Vivaldi

The Joy of Creation:
The Story of Clara Schumann

Library of Congress Cataloging-in-Publication Data

Shichtman, Sandra H.
    The Joy of Creation : The Story of Clara Schumann / by Sandra
        Shichtman and Dorothy Indenbaum. p. cm. --
        (Classical composers)
    Includes bibliographical references and index.
    ISBN 978-1-59935-123-0 (alk. paper)
 1. Schumann, Clara, 1819-1896--Juvenile literature. 2. Pianists
    -Germany--Biography--Juvenile literature. 3. Composers--
    Germany--Biography--Juvenile literature. I. Indenbaum, Dorothy.
    II. Title.
    ML3930.S385S55 2010
    786.2092--dc22
    [B]
                                            2009054289

Printed in the United States of America
First Edition

- Sandra -
To my husband, Michael, the wind beneath my wings

- Dorothy -
To my loving son, Arthur

Contents

CHAPTER 1

Waiting for Something to Say

I t was 1823, and four-year-old Clara Wieck hadn't spoken a word in her young life. Her parents assumed the worst. Their daughter must be deaf, a sad outcome for the child of a noted musician and teacher such as Friedrich Wieck. But not only was there nothing wrong with young Clara's ears, her lifelong ability to hear, create, and play music would eventually make her one of history's remarkable musical figures.

Clara, one of the great pianists of the nineteenth century, would be cheered by audiences from the royal courts of England and Russia to countless halls and private homes throughout Europe.

She would compose an impressive collection of music. Among her published works are piano pieces—polonaises, caprices, romances, and waltzes. She set poems by well-known poets to music and wrote preludes and fugues, romances for piano and violin, a Trio for Piano, Violin and

Cello—considered her finest work—and cadenzas for Beethoven's *Piano Concerto in C Minor* and for Mozart's *Piano Concerto in D Minor*. Her unpublished works included pieces for voice and piano, as well as pieces for solo piano.

How Clara made her way from an uncertain beginning as a quiet toddler to become an international music superstar is a story filled with personal and professional ups and downs.

Clara Josephine Wieck was born in Leipzig, Germany, on September 13, 1819, to Friedrich and Marianne Wieck. She was the second of five children. An older child, Adelheid, had died on May 12, 1818, at the age of nine months. She later gained two younger brothers; Alwin, born on August 27, 1821, and Gustav, born January 31, 1823. A third brother, Victor, died on January 2, 1827, at age three.

Her father, Friedrich Wieck, was born August 18, 1785, in the small town of Pretzsch, about twenty-eight miles from Leipzig. His family was poor. Except for young Friedrich, they had no interest in music. He was highly intelligent and dedicated to his work. He studied religion at the University of Wittenberg, working his way through college as a tutor and supporting himself that way for nine years. But he didn't become a minister as he had planned. Instead, he followed his first love and became a musician.

With borrowed money, Wieck set up a piano store in Leipzig where he loaned pieces of music and sold, rented, and repaired pianos. Leipzig was a center of music at the time, so Wieck was able to meet many musicians who came through the city. In 1815, he began to give piano lessons.

At the time, Leipzig was recovering from the Napoleonic Wars. People of the middle class, who now had money to spend, wanted pianos and piano lessons. Friedrich Wieck was in the

right place at the right time with the right products and, as a result, he became very successful.

He soon fell in love with one of his students, nineteen-year-old Marianne Tromlitz. She was born on May 17, 1797, in Plauen, a town south of Leipzig. Unlike Wieck, Marianne was born into a musical family. Her father sang profession-ally. Her grandfather, a well-known flutist, was also a music teacher and flute maker.

Friedrich Wieck and Marianne Tromlitz were married on June 23, 1816. Wieck was thirty-one years old at the time. Marianne was a professional soprano singer and concert pia-nist. A review in the music journal *Allgemeine musikalische Zeitung* of her performance at the Leipzig *Gewandhaus* soon after her marriage praised her "skill, confidence, and dil-igence." Her talents, and the fact that Wieck had been her teacher, made him highly esteemed as a piano teacher.

After her marriage, Marianne Wieck performed in con-certs at the Leipzig *Gewandhaus*, gave birth to five children in only seven years, ran a household, and gave piano and voice lessons.

There was always music in the Wieck house. Customers tried out the pianos in the shop, students took their lessons, and Marianne Wieck practiced for her per-formances. Despite her lack of early speaking skills,

Clara's hometown of Leipzig, Germany

Clara apparently never had any trouble hearing the music that went on all around her.

The family took long walks every day. When Clara was three, she was allowed to join them. Her parents walked very fast and she was expected to keep up with their pace. Wieck believed that exercise in the fresh air was important to a person's health and well-being. Clara continued this practice of walking briskly throughout her life.

Unfortunately, the marriage between Friedrich and Marianne was not a happy one. Although intelligent and hardworking, Wieck was often demanding, impatient, and stubborn. Marianne Wieck left her husband in 1824, when Clara was five years old. She had had enough of his bad temper and the constant arguments in the house. She returned to her hometown, Plauen, and sought a divorce.

It was unusual in the nineteenth century for a woman to divorce her husband, because she was considered his property. As a result, Marianne was entirely at the mercy of her husband. She had to give up her children, who also were considered their father's property, in order to get a divorce.

The divorce was granted on January 22, 1825, and in August Marianne married Adolph Bargiel, a music teacher, who had been a friend of the Wiecks. She lived in Leipzig with her new husband for about a year before Bargiel took a job in Berlin.

Clara and her baby brother Victor lived with their mother for a short time after she left the Wieck house. But, once the divorce was finalized, Clara returned to live permanently with her father and brothers. As long as the Bargiels lived in Leipzig, Wieck allowed the children to visit their mother. But, with her mother's move to Berlin, Clara lost the affection and influence of one of the most important women in a little girl's life.

At the same time, her father fired their servant Johanna Strobel, the other important woman in Clara's life.

Her father started Clara's piano lessons when she was five. He was convinced he could train her to become a piano virtuoso, or an expert performer. He started with short pieces, some of which he adapted from existing works, others composed especially for Clara. She learned them quickly. It appeared she had an excellent memory and could play a piece after hearing it only once. Even before Clara spoke normally or appeared to understand words, Wieck realized she had no trouble hearing music.

Wieck also started a diary for her, a fortunate decision for later generations studying the life of Clara. Wieck wrote on the first page, "My Diary, begun by my Father, the 7th of June 1827 and to be continued by Clara Josephine Wieck." Since Clara couldn't yet write, her father did it for her, writing in first person as if Clara were making the entries.

One early entry described Clara's first piano lessons. "On September 18th, my father began to give me regular piano lessons. Already, some months before my mother took me with her to Plauen, I had learned to play several exercises without moving the hand and had picked up a few simple dance tunes by ear, but this is all that I could accomplish since I could neither speak myself nor understand others."

That winter her father took Clara to a concert at the *Gewandhaus* for the first time. The diary read, "I heard a grand symphony of Beethoven's, amongst other things, which excited me greatly. Also I heard some big choral works, which interested me very much." A few weeks later, Wieck took his daughter to the theater.

When she reached six, Clara started school, but she attended only for a short time. After that she was tutored at home.

Her father explained his views on the education of his children in an article he wrote years later: "My daughters always had a special tutor with whom I worked so that with just a few hours a day, their general education could keep pace with their artistic training and still leave enough time to exercise outdoors and strengthen their bodies, while other children have to sweat for nine hours a day on school benches and pay for this with the loss of their health and happy childhood."

Ludwig van Beethoven, who Clara admired and featured in her concerts

Each day, Clara received a music lesson from her father, then practiced for two hours. Being a small child, Clara was eager to please her father and happy to have him all to herself during the lessons. Wieck encouraged her to compose small musical pieces of her own, and, by the time she was seven, Clara was giving concerts in her own home. Students, family members, and servants were brought in to listen. Soon afterward, her father began taking Clara to concerts, plays, and operas regularly.

In 1827 Wieck ordered a piano for Clara from Vienna. By that time she could distinguish the different sounds of the piano keys. Her father, pretending to be Clara, wrote in the diary, "My perception of music began to develop more and more quickly, and I could distinguish the keys with fair certainty simply by ear." Clara's playing had improved to the point that she could play long, difficult pieces. He often praised her for her ability, praise that Clara enjoyed receiving. Over time, Wieck increased Clara's daily practice from two to three hours and began to teach her music theory, which is the study of the sounds of music and how they go together.

On September 9, 1827, Clara played Mozart's E-major concerto before a selected audience at a concert rehearsal. She wrote to her mother in Berlin, "Everything went quite well and I didn't get stuck. Only my cadenza [a musical passage performed by the soloist] wouldn't come off right away . . . yet it didn't scare me at all."

The next February Clara played a duet with her father at a musical evening in their home that was attended by many people. On March 31, she played at the home of a local doctor, Dr. Carus, after which her diary reported, "I made fewer mistakes than the gentlemen who accompanied me."

She began to develop a reputation by performing in the homes of wealthy patrons during this time. In response, she received gifts of clothing, jewelry, and money from them. As her confidence grew, Clara became accustomed to wearing beautiful gowns. She clearly enjoyed the excitement and thrills of performing, and being applauded and praised.

After several private performances at the homes of family and friends, Clara made her public debut on October 20, 1828, at age nine at the Leipzig *Gewandhaus*, the most famous concert hall in Leipzig. During the brief appearance Clara played a piano duet with another girl, Emilie Reichold, who was also a student of Wieck's. Clara wrote in her diary about

An audience leaving the Leipzig *Gewandhaus* after a concert
(Courtesy of Lebrecht Music and Arts Photo Library / Alamy)

her performance, "It went very well, and I did not play any wrong notes, but got much applause."

On the day of the performance, Wieck went to the *Gewandhaus* ahead of Clara to make certain everything was ready. The *Gewandhaus* planned to send a coach to bring Clara to the concert hall in time for her performance. When a coach arrived in front of the Wieck house, looking for Fraulein Clara, she got into the coach. She realized that she didn't know the other girls in the coach, and when the coach headed in the wrong direction, away from the *Gewandhaus*, Clara became alarmed. It turned out that this coach had picked up the wrong Fraulein Clara. Another girl with the same first name, who was being taken to a party, lived in the Wiecks' apartment building. A distraught Clara returned home to await the proper coach. When it arrived, Clara got into it and arrived at the concert hall on time.

Wieck knew that he had to calm Clara right away or she would be too upset to perform. The quick-thinking Wieck told her, "I quite forgot to tell you Clarchen [Darling Clara], that people are always taken to the wrong house, the first time they play in public."

The exaggeration must have worked to settle Clara's nerves. The *Gewandhaus* audience responded enthusiastically and with great applause. Both she and her father received favorable reviews in the press from reviewers who attended the performance.

Nine-year-old Clara Wieck had her first success as a pianist. It was a sign of big things ahead.

CHAPTER 2

Child Prodigy

In spring 1830, as a result of the favorable notices and reactions from audiences in Leipzig, Friedrich and Clara Wieck traveled by coach to Dresden for her first appearances outside her hometown. Wieck wanted Clara to meet people and establish new relationships.

The trip was successful for daughter and father. Clara gave several private performances, and Wieck received many offers to give piano lessons. For a short time he even thought about moving his family to Dresden, where he felt he would be more appreciated. Poking fun at himself and at Leipzig audiences, he wrote to his second wife, Clementine Fechner, whom he had recently married, "The sensation the two apes [Clara and himself] from the Leipzig menagerie are making here is not to be described. In Leipzig, they are too amazed and too nasty . . . to realize what an extraordinary child Clara is, and even less that your Fritz from Pretzsch [Wieck] could possess and educate this very same Clara." Clara was playing, he said,

Clara Wieck
(Courtesy of The Art Archive / Alamy)

with a self-confidence she had never shown before, although her personality remained unchanged.

Clara spent that summer at home in Leipzig learning the music of Frederic Chopin and developing her musical understanding of his works. Her diary revealed the difficulty she had with one piece. "Chopin's Variations Op. 2, which I learned [sic] in eight days, is the most difficult piece of music which I have ever seen or played." But, since she *had* mastered it, she planned to play it for the first time at the next concert she'd give, whether in Leipzig or Berlin.

That summer a young man, Robert Schumann, came to Leipzig to study piano with Wieck. Schumann had taken lessons from Wieck a few years earlier, when he'd been a law student at the University in Leipzig. Now he wanted to become a concert pianist and Wieck was a well-known piano teacher.

Robert Schumann was born on June 8, 1810, in Zwickau, Germany, about eighty miles south of Leipzig. He was the youngest of five children of August and Johanna Schumann.

August Schumann was a bookseller in Zwickau. He recognized his son's interest in music and arranged for the boy to study piano. He also noted his son's love of literature. But when it was time for Robert to go to the university, his mother insisted that he study law. Robert enrolled as a law student, but he preferred music and literature and spent more time reading and making music than he did studying law. He also liked to spend time with his friends in a drinking establishment, something Wieck found disturbing and later used against Robert.

Because Robert wanted to become a musician instead of a lawyer, he begged his mother to allow him to study with the eminent Friedrich Wieck. Johanna Schumann wrote to ask Wieck if he thought her son could become a successful

concert pianist. Wieck assured her that he could make a musician of her son within a short time. In October 1830 Robert
moved into the Wieck home and began taking piano lessons.

Although Robert was nine years older than the oldest
Wieck child, Clara, he had not forgotten what it was like to
be a child. He brought joy and laughter into the house. He
entertained the children, played games with them, told them
ghost stories, "and played charades with them; he teased and
frolicked and had the little boys taking turns standing on one
leg—the one who could hold out the longest received a prize."

Clara was preparing for her first solo performance when
Robert moved into their home. She gave that performance
on November 8, 1830, at the Leipzig *Gewandhaus* when she
was just eleven years old. Both the review and the money she
earned were good. A Leipzig reviewer wrote, "This young
artist's extraordinary accomplishment, in her playing as well
as her composing, led to general astonishment and the greatest applause." The reviewer also praised Wieck for his excellent piano instruction.

That year, Clara composed her first piano compositions,
Quatre Polonaises pour le Pianoforte (*Four Polish Dances
for the Piano*). The compositions were published the following year in Leipzig and sold in music stores.

Her initial successes encouraged her father to give up
his business and his other students and devote himself to his
daughter's musical career. He left his business and students
in the capable hands of his wife, then pregnant with their first
child. Wieck planned to take Clara on an extended tour that
would include concerts in various German cities and in Paris.

Since the late eighteenth century, singers had been touring with opera companies. Audiences filled the opera houses,

and pianists and violinists found that they could earn a living there, too, through extended tours that often lasted for months.

Young Clara needed to add more piano pieces to her repertoire. She began work on her second group of piano pieces, *Caprices en forme de valse Pour le Piano* (*Caprices in the form of a Waltz for the Piano*) in 1831. Caprices are humorous, imaginative pieces. Clara completed the work the following year, and it was published in both Paris and Leipzig.

Paris was the center of the music world at the time, so it was natural that Wieck would take Clara there to perform. Prior to their leaving Leipzig to begin the tour, her father insisted that she learn French.

Robert Schumann
at age thirty

Unfortunately, the tour was delayed for a while because of a cholera outbreak in Berlin, one of the cities on the scheduled tour. Cholera was one of the most feared diseases of the nineteenth century because there was no cure for the highly contagious intestinal disease. People who got sick became dehydrated and died, sometimes in just a few hours. Cholera killed thousands of people as it made its way from Asia to Western Europe in the early 1830s. After the epidemic was over in Berlin, Clara and her father left Leipzig on September 25, 1831. They stopped first in Weimar, a day's journey by coach from Leipzig. On October 1 they visited the home of Johann Wolfgang von Goethe, the well-known poet and writer.

Clara's diary describes the scene at Goethe's home: "We found him reading and the servant took us in without further announcement, as he had made an appointment with us the day before for this hour." Goethe welcomed them and asked Clara to sit next to him on the sofa. Then he asked her to play the piano for him and his family. When he realized that Clara was too small to reach the piano keys, Goethe put a cushion on the piano stool for her.

Goethe "admired Clara's intelligent rendering" of the pieces she played. Once it became known that Clara had won his approval, everyone in Weimar wanted to see her play, and a concert was hastily arranged for October 7.

Two days after the concert, Goethe invited Clara to return to his home and play for him again. Later, she received a gift from the poet. It was a medal with a portrait of Goethe on it and a note that read, "To the gifted Clara Wieck."

Father and daughter left Weimar on October 10 and continued the concert tour in other German cities on their way to Paris. It was the start of Clara's lifelong career of touring and giving concerts.

When they arrived in Frankfurt, Wieck learned that his wife had given birth to a daughter, Marie, on January 17, 1832. There were also letters waiting from Robert Schumann, who wrote to Wieck, "In the first place, please accept my best wishes for Clara's success . . . . You would hardly believe how much I miss you and her."

Robert's letter to Clara spoke of books he had read while she was away. "I have been in Arabia during your absence, in order to be able to relate all the fairy-tales which might please you—six new stories of doubles, 101 charades, 8 amusing riddles, as well as the lovely, horrible robber-stories and that of the white ghost—ugh, ugh! How I am shaking!" He included news about Clara's brothers, writing that Alwin had become handsome and now dressed the way Robert did in a new blue coat and leather cap. Robert wrote that Clara's brother Gustav had grown nearly as tall as Robert.

Clara gave several successful concerts in Frankfurt. At one, she included a piece that she had composed based on *Der Traum* (*The Dream*), a poem by Christoph August Tiedge.

On the tour, Wieck booked the hotel rooms, ordered their food, contacted music people who could be helpful, rented the concert hall, made certain the piano was properly tuned, had programs printed, publicized the concert, and collected the money that it generated. He saw to it that Clara copied all of the pertinent information about each concert into her diary—in essence, teaching her the business of managing a concert tour.

After all of the expenses had been paid, her father gave Clara a small amount of money as a gift for having performed well. He kept the rest of the money as payment for having given up his business and students in order to promote Clara's career.

At every stop, Clara performed, practiced, studied new compositions to add to her repertoire, composed, and studied French. Among the new compositions was Chopin's variations on Mozart's aria from his opera *Don Giovanni, "La ci darem la mano"* ("Give me your hand"). Her father had discovered it the previous summer and realized it would be a perfect addition to Clara's repertoire because it would show off her talent.

Clara and her father finally arrived in Paris on February 15, 1832. Clara's uncle, Eduard Fechner, had rented rooms for them at the Hotel de Bergere. Wieck had only a few contacts in Paris, so he relied on Fechner to make introductions and arrange Clara's first few concerts in the salons of wealthy Parisian women.

In the nineteenth century it was traditional for women of the upper class to give concerts in their salons, or parlors. They were, for the most part, confined to their homes and not allowed to work or to travel without mature companionship. Their salons were their "window" to the world outside their homes, so they invited writers, politicians, and musicians, as well as their family and friends, to these concerts. Their guests brought news of what was going on in the world. The women hired both musicians and singers for these concerts.

For Clara, several public concerts followed. In March 1832 a reviewer for the music journal *Allgemeine musikalische Zeitung* wrote,

> *Even in her first piece, the artist who is still so young reaped thundering approval that mounted to enthusiasm in the works that followed. And indeed, the great skill, assurance, and strength with which she plays even the most difficult movements so easily is highly remarkable.*

The cholera epidemic reached Paris during the Wiecks' visit there. As a result, fewer people went out in public for fear they would catch the disease. Clara's April 9 concert at the Hotel de Ville, which had a large room suitable for a concert, was held in a smaller room instead because of poor ticket sales. It was the last concert on the tour. Father and daughter left Paris on April 13 and reached Leipzig on May 1.

Robert Schumann was there to welcome them home. He had missed his teacher and his young friend Clara during their absence. In the days that followed their departure, he wrote about Clara several times in his diary. Later, he added, "Clara arrived early yesterday with Wieck. Gustav and Alwin [her brothers] came to let me know immediately." The next day he wrote, "Clara is prettier and taller, stronger and more skilled and has acquired a French accent when she speaks German."

Clara continued to learn new pieces and to compose. In 1833, she composed her third group of piano pieces, *Romance varie* (*Romance with Variations*). They were published during the summer in Leipzig and Paris.

By the time she reached adolescence, Clara's sunny personality began to change. She became moody and rebellious. One moment she was a mature young woman; the next, she reverted to childishness. Robert wrote in his diary, "Clara is stubborn, and a cry-baby. Her father has to scold her, but she has him under her slipper. She is dominating . . . but then again she can plead and wheedle like a child."

Wieck noticed the change in his daughter. The once docile and obedient little girl no longer obeyed him. She was less enthusiastic about practicing the piano and preferred sleeping late and receiving visitors. When asked to play the piano, Clara was not enthusiastic about doing so. In the past, she had always been compliant and eager to please him. Now, she was becoming a typical teenager and Wieck did not know how to handle her.

Still, Clara was his most talented student and he devoted more of his time to her training than to any other student. Her talent was beginning to be noticed and appreciated. She brought money into the household; she brought her father prestige and fame because he was the teacher of a child prodigy.

Clara also began to show an interest in boys in general and one in particular—Robert Schumann. This made Wieck even more nervous. Perhaps she would not want to perform in the future, especially if she were to marry. To separate Clara and Robert, Wieck sent his daughter to Dresden to study singing and instrumentation, so that, in the future, she could compose orchestral music.

While Clara was in Dresden, Robert began to go out with Ernestine von Fricken, a former student of Wieck's who was now his wife's student. Robert became secretly engaged to her in August 1834.

Clara was upset when she found out about the engagement. She had fallen in love with Robert. Now, he was engaged to marry someone else.

The Hotel de Ville, where Clara performed in Paris during the cholera epidemic in 1832

But the engagement did not last. When Ernestine's father became ill in September, she returned home to care for him. While Ernestine was away from Leipzig, Robert became interested in Clara, who had returned from Dresden in July 1834. He decided to break off his engagement to Ernestine and courted Clara instead.

By 1835 Clara was acknowledged throughout Europe as a phenomenally talented child prodigy, although still only sixteen. Continuing to perform and compose music helped Clara both to express her deepest emotions and to develop as a musician.

That year she wrote several compositions, *Valses romantiques* (*Romantic Waltzes*) and *Quatre pieces characteristiques* (*Four Characteristic Pieces*). The latter were called *Le Sabbat* (*The Sabbath*), *Caprice a la Bolero* (an imaginative piece based on the bolero, a Spanish dance), *Romance*, and *Ballet des Revenants* (*Ballet about Ghosts*).

In November Clara received her first romantic kiss from Robert on the front stairs of her house. She was surprised and excited. She wrote to Robert, "When you gave me that first kiss, I thought I would faint; everything went blank and I could barely hold the lamp that was lighting your way out."

When Wieck again noticed the attraction between Clara and Robert, he forbade contact between the two and tried to keep them from seeing each other. He took Clara on another concert tour in Germany, both to keep her from Robert and to earn money for the family. Since it was important for her to include new material in her concerts, Clara continued to compose. She wrote *Soirees Musicales* (*Musical Evenings*), which she dedicated to her friend, Henriette Voigt. The composition was published that year in Leipzig and Paris.

For the next year-and-a-half Wieck's plan to separate Clara from Robert was successful. They had no contact, sending no letters to each other nor meeting in person. Clara spent most of the time away from Leipzig on concert tours, while Robert remained in the city and worked on his music journal, *Neue Zeitschrift fur Musik* (*New Journal for Music*), which he and friends had started in 1834.

Early in February 1836 Clara performed in Dresden. When Wieck left Clara there with friends and returned to Leipzig on business, Robert came to Dresden. He and Clara met secretly. When Wieck found out, he threatened to shoot Robert if he

The *Frauenkirche*, or Church of Our Lady, in Dresden, Germany
(*Courtesy of iStockphoto.com*)

ever approached Clara again. He felt that Robert was not good enough to marry his daughter. Marriage between the two young people would not be suitable, he believed, since Clara was a successful pianist and Robert had not yet gained much recognition as a composer, editor, or music journalist. Clara's future needs would be substantial if she was to continue her career as a pianist and composer.

He demanded that Clara return Robert's letters and retrieve the ones she had sent to him. Clara, who loved and obeyed her father, did as she was told.

It seemed Wieck had succeeded in keeping Clara and Robert apart permanently. But love would find a way.

CHAPTER 3

The Secret Engagement

During the next year Friedrich Wieck continued to try to keep his daughter and his former student apart. He criticized Robert, telling Clara that if she married him her career as a concert pianist would be over. Clara tried her best to defend her beloved, but she didn't want to antagonize her father either.

Finally, her father threatened to disown her if she married Robert. In spite of this threat, Clara and Robert managed to meet secretly and fell deeply in love. They were determined not to let Clara's father become suspicious, so they developed a system for exchanging letters secretly. They sent their letters to trusted friends, who put them into new envelopes and sent them on to the post office. Then Clara's trusted maid picked up Robert's letters for her. On August 14, 1837, the couple considered themselves engaged secretly and exchanged rings to commemorate the engagement.

On Clara's eighteenth birthday, September 13, 1837, Robert formally asked Wieck for permission to marry his daughter. Wieck refused, on the grounds that Robert would not be able to provide for Clara. He feared that Clara would give up performing and the couple would have to live on Robert's meager income.

The battle lines were drawn between Wieck and the couple. It would become increasingly fierce and go on for two years.

At the same time, Clara continued to perform and compose. She composed *Variations de Concret pour le Pianoforte sur la Cavatine du Pirate de Bellini* (*Piano Variations on a Theme from the Opera Pirate by Bellini*) in 1837.

That winter, Clara started her first concert tour to Vienna, Austria, accompanied by her father. It was a huge success. Both musicians and members of the Austrian emperor's court adored the young German pianist. The emperor called her *wundermadchen* (wonder girl). In March 1838, she received Austria's highest honor, an appointment as Royal and Imperial Virtuosa.

Wieck was overjoyed at the honor. He felt that, as Clara's teacher, he was honored as well. He wrote, "What a letter of recommendation this is! What a lesson to the envious pianists who have made a public spectacle of all my aspirations." His hard work as Clara's teacher was finally being rewarded, and Wieck hoped that she would now understand the necessity of maintaining a vigorous practice and performing schedule.

Clara began to include in her concerts Robert's compositions *Carnaval* and Sonata in F sharp minor. In this way, she introduced his music to audiences who had never heard it before, therefore adding to his reputation as a composer. It was a habit Clara Schumann would continue throughout her career.

Despite his misgivings about the engagement, her father expected Robert to write about Clara in *Neue Zeitschrift für Musik* to show that he was grateful that she was playing his music. When Robert didn't mention that he would do so, Wieck became angry at the young man's lack of appreciation. It was one more reason why Wieck would not give permission for Clara to marry Robert.

The Imperial Palace in Vienna, Austria, where Clara performed for the Austrian emperor
(Courtesy of Andrew Bossi)

While in Vienna, Clara rehearsed and performed concerts for appreciative audiences. People came up to speak with her after the performances. Afterward, she often played at the homes of influential people, returning late to her lodgings. When she could, she sent a short letter to Robert to tell him about the concerts and about audiences' reactions to his works.

Clara knew her father would become angry if he came upon her writing to Robert. She understood how her father felt about her marrying anyone at all. "I am very upset when I see how miserable Father is when he thinks of losing me someday—I know my duty toward him and yet I love you endlessly," she told Robert.

However, she was ambivalent. Should her loyalty be to her father, who had given her everything she had, who had spent many hours training her to be a concert pianist? Or should it be to Robert, whom she loved more than anyone else, whom she would never stop loving? The problem weighed heavily on her mind.

Although Robert understood Clara's love for her father, and tried to be patient, his feelings were hurt by her ambivalence. He urged her to decide. "You are, forgive me, like a pair of children," Robert wrote to Clara. "You cry, he scolds, and it is still the same as ever. . . . You can't belong to him and to me at the same time. You will have to leave one, him or me."

But Clara knew that her father's concern for her future was valid. She wrote to Robert that she, too, was thinking about her future. Clara was used to having a career and maintaining a certain standard of living, and she was not ready to give up either when she married.

Clara's words echoed some of her father's comments about Robert's low economic status. Many letters were sent between

Leipzig and Vienna on the subject of whether or not the marriage would take place. Finally, Robert became so frustrated with Clara's inability to make a decision that he wrote, "since you value my ring so little, I care no longer for yours, since yesterday, and do not wear it. I dreamed that I was walking by deep water—and an impulse seized me and I threw the ring into the water—and then I was filled with a passionate longing to plunge in after it."

As he intended, the letter hurt Clara. But its last, strange sentence also foreshadowed a terrible tragedy that would unfold in the coming years.

As Clara continued to perform in Vienna, Robert complained that she did not write to him often enough. He was unsure that she still loved him.

Clara blamed her busy schedule. "How much one has to do in order to bring away a few thaler [German money] from a town. While you are sitting with Poppe [a drinking establishment in Leipzig] at 10 o'clock in the evening, or are going home, I, poor thing, am arriving at a party, where I have to play to people for a few pretty words and a cup of warm water, and get home, dead tired, at 11 or 12 o'clock, drink a draught [small amount] of water, lie down."

At one point during the tour, Clara mistakenly believed that her father had changed his mind and felt more favorably toward Robert. She happily wrote to Robert, "I talked to Father a great deal about you to-day, and he told me that he was quite inclined to be friendly to you when we came back; you are to be the friend of the house again."

But her father had other plans. He imposed a condition that he thought would keep the marriage from ever taking place. He insisted that that the couple earn at least 2,000 thaler a year before they married. Wieck intentionally set the number so high in the hope that Clara and Robert would not reach it.

But, the young couple looked at this condition in a different light. At last, they thought, here was something concrete. If they could show Clara's father that their total worth was at least 2,000 thaler a year, perhaps he would let them get married.

Clara began to plan how to earn the most money in the shortest time. She thought about giving more concerts, especially in Vienna, because of how well she had been received there. She even thought that she and Robert would leave Leipzig after their marriage and settle in Vienna. "I can give a concert every winter which will bring me 1000 thaler (easily)," she wrote. "Then I can, and will, give a lesson every day, that will bring in another 1000 thaler during the year." With the 1,000 thaler Robert earned, Clara was convinced that they would meet her father's requirement.

She also proposed that they postpone their marriage until after 1840, when she would be twenty-one and could marry without her father's consent.

Little did the young couple know that Friedrich Wieck had plans to ensure that the marriage would never happen. When the Vienna tour was over, he and Clara returned to Leipzig. There, Wieck continued to speak negatively about Robert to Clara and to people he knew.

By late November, Clara had enough. "For your sake I will give up my father, whom I love more than anyone except for you. I will follow you without my father's consent," she wrote to Robert.

Again, Clara's father had something else in mind. He arranged a concert tour in Paris for his daughter, but said he would not accompany her unless she gave Robert up. The thought of traveling without her father frightened Clara. Unmarried women in Europe in the nineteenth century did not travel alone. In Clara's case her father not only acted as her escort, but also made the concert and lodging arrangements. He introduced her to important people in the world of music. Yet the thought of canceling the concert tour never entered Clara's mind. Even when Robert strongly suggested that she not go, Clara refused to cancel the trip.

When she insisted she would go without him, her father hired a French woman, Claudine Dufourd, to accompany his daughter. Clara felt uncomfortable about traveling with a stranger. She wanted her devoted nanny to go with them, but Friedrich refused to allow it. Clara left Leipzig in a snowstorm on January 8, 1839.

Wieck hoped the trip would be a disastrous failure, and Clara would realize how important he was to her career and choose him over Robert. Clara, on the other hand, convinced herself that her father had business to attend to but would join her as soon as he was able to leave Leipzig.

As in the past, she gave concerts in German towns along the way, including successful ones in Nuremberg, Stuttgart, and Karlesruhe. After all expenses were paid, Clara had enough money to continue on to Paris. While in Stuttgart, Clara met Henriette Reichmann, a young woman close in age to Clara. Henriette asked Clara if she could travel with her to Paris, where she wanted to study the piano. Clara liked Henriette immediately and was delighted to have her as a travel companion.

The two arrived in Paris on February 6, 1839. Clara renewed acquaintances with musicians and composers she

had met during her first trip there in 1832. She met many new people from the musical world and sought their advice on how to arrange concerts, rent pianos, and find lodgings—the things that her father had done for her in the past.

Clara still expected her father to join her. But a week after her arrival, her father still hadn't arrived. She received several letters from him in which Wieck offered only advice and reproach about her trip to Paris—but no date on which he would come.

Clara's expectations faded to hope, then disbelief. He never came to Paris. And he continued to refuse consent for a marriage between his daughter and his former student.

But Clara had learned well from her father and now proved to be a capable young woman. She was able to arrange her own tour and maintain the high musical standards her father had instilled in her, despite the emotional stress of Wieck's absence and his refusal to allow her marriage. It was a big turning point in Clara's personal life and professional career.

She decided there was nothing to do but to petition the court in Leipzig to allow her and Robert to marry without Wieck's permission once she turned twenty-one. On June

The Arc de Triomphe in Paris
(Courtesy of Benh Lieu Song)

15, 1839, Clara signed her name to the marriage petition, which Robert had already signed, and sent it to the Court of Appeals in Leipzig. Their fate was now in the hands of the court. Would the court give its permission for Clara and Robert to marry?

When Wieck received word that the petition had been filed, he was furious. He locked his daughter out of the house in Leipzig without her belongings—clothes, books, and piano. He refused to give her any of her concert earnings.

Clara had no way of knowing that this act of independence would help her face future difficulties, tragedies, and heart-break in life with strength and dignity.

While waiting for news from the court, Clara stayed at the home of friends in Leipzig for a while; then she went to Berlin to live with her mother and stepfather. Although the family was poor and there were young children in the house, Marianne Bargiel made her oldest daughter feel at home. She even traveled with Clara as her chaperone when Clara performed in other German cities.

Wieck asked the court for time to present more evidence to the court. There, he spoke unfavorably about Robert, accusing him of drinking excessively and of being interested in Clara only because of the money she earned.

In her diary Clara described the scene in the courtroom. "I could not look at my father in court without feeling a deep sense of compassion . . . . He burst into violent fits of rage, and several times the judge had to order him to be silent. I shuddered each time this happened, and could scarcely bear to see him subjected to such humiliation . . . . My heart too feels as though it has been torn apart." Clara realized that her emotional bond with her father was forever broken.

Clara and Robert Shchumann

In contrast to Wieck's anger in court, Robert remained calm and conducted himself in what Clara thought was a gentlemanly manner. She was proud of him for enduring Wieck's insults and felt more in love with him than ever.

After the young couple proved Wieck's accusations false, the court ruled in their favor. On August 1, 1840, it gave Clara and Robert permission to marry, and the couple posted their *banns*, a public announcement of the upcoming marriage, two weeks later.

Clara gave her last concert as Clara Wieck on September 5, 1840, in Weimar. She and her beloved Robert were married in the church at Schonefeld on September 12, 1840, the day before her twenty-first birthday. They settled in Leipzig.

The secret engagement had come to an end.

CHAPTER 4

The Early Years of Marriage

After Clara and Robert Schumann married, they began a diary in which both wrote. Clara wrote in it one week and Robert wrote in it the next week. On the first page, he wrote, "This book which I open today . . . is to be a record of all that concerns us in our home life and marriage; our dreams and hopes are to find expression here, as well as those things we would tell each other."

They included comments about their music and people they met. They wrote about problems that came up and made suggestions for dealing with them and for improving their marriage.

After a while, when Robert became deeply absorbed by his work, it fell to Clara alone to write in the diary. In December, she wrote, "We have been married a quarter of a year today, and it is the happiest quarter of a year of my life."

On March 31, 1841, Clara gave her first concert as a married woman. She performed at the Leipzig *Gewandhaus*, where she premiered her husband's *Spring Symphony* arranged for the piano.

Clara's return to the concert hall was an enormous success. She described the audience's reaction and her own emotions in a letter to her friend Emilie List, a student of her father's. "I was received with such enthusiasm that I went pale and red; it did not cease even when I seated myself at the piano . . . . You can imagine that this gave me courage since I had been shaking all over with anxiety. I played as I can hardly ever remember playing."

Emilie was the daughter of a German diplomat with whom Clara became friends when Emilie took piano lessons from Friedrich Wieck. They remained friends throughout Clara's life.

By this time the Schumanns were expecting their first child, but Clara knew that she had to continue to perform. She had an intense musical drive and loved the applause and admiration she received from audiences.

She also needed the money she received from her concerts to pay the household expenses. That meant traveling both to German cities and other countries. Otherwise audiences would soon forget about her, something she could not allow to happen.

One dark cloud marred Clara's happiness: she and her father no longer communicated directly. Their only contact was through the court, where Robert had filed a slander suit against Wieck because of lies about his son-in-law. The suit wasn't settled until April 1841.

By then, Wieck had relocated to Dresden, but he continued to spread lies about Clara and her husband. He did not respond to the birthday greetings she sent him in August 1841.

Clara Wieck.

k. k. oesterreichifche Kammer-Virtuosinn.

Clara Weick Schumann

And when Clara sent word that her first child, Marie, was born on September 1, he responded with a rude letter.

Clara resumed her performances later that year with concerts in Weimar. Since the city was close to Leipzig, she went without her husband. He remained at home with baby Marie, who was cared for by servants.

Later, when Clara needed to go to Hamburg to perform, her husband accompanied her while Marie stayed at home with servants. Robert expected that he would have time to compose and to write while his wife performed. But he found he did not like to travel and could not compose while he was away from home. His job as an editor required his attention at home as well.

Robert also believed that Marie was too young to be without her parents for the long period of time a tour required. Being cared for by servants was not the same as being cared for by at least one parent. Before long, Robert returned home

The Nyhavn Canal in Copenhagen, Denmark
(*Courtesy of Scythian*)

to Leipzig to tend to his daughter. In the nineteenth century it was uncommon for a father to be this involved with his child's well-being.

Clara gave more than a dozen concerts during the first few months of 1842. In March, when she left Leipzig to go to Copenhagen, Denmark, Robert did not go with her. Her father spread the word that this was because Clara and her husband had separated.

While Clara was away Robert wrote to tell her how depressed he felt that she was not with him. He also told her, "I wanted to write to you yesterday, but was so sick with a horrible anger that I could not. Your father has told all of Dresden that we *were separated*. On many days . . . one can laugh at such baseness, but on others it can embitter the heart and I have had many days like that."

Wieck also lied about the Schumanns' visit to Hamburg the previous year. Clara received a letter in which Robert told her

he'd heard from someone there "that I'd left you in Hamburg *sick*—that we ran up debts in Hamburg, that nobody liked you there, and all sorts of things like that." He asked his wife to put the gossip to rest with excellent performances and her usual artistry.

Clara explained her decision to go to Copenhagen without her husband to her friend Emilie when she returned to Leipzig. "I earn nothing at home, why should I not by means of my talent, gain my mite for Robert? Could anyone think ill of me for so doing, or of my husband for going home to his child and his business?"

The determined young woman set out for Copenhagen, which required her to travel by boat as well as by coach. Clara had never traveled by boat, and the overnight sea journey frightened her. Later, a storm arose and the journey

Copenhagen, Denmark, circa 1890
(Courtesy of the Library of Congress)

had to be delayed until the weather was more favorable. Clara quickly arranged to give several concerts until the weather cleared.

The Copenhagen tour was a success. Clara gave more than a half-dozen well-attended concerts, which brought her a good amount of money. She met the Danish royal family and, on her return home, dedicated a new composition to the Danish queen.

Although Clara was comfortable touring without Robert, he felt ambivalent about not accompanying her. He was also afraid that his career was keeping her from realizing her full potential as a musician. Both Clara and Robert acknowledged that, because of their genders, her career took a back seat to his. His letters to her reflected his conflicting emotions. While she was in Copenhagen, he wrote to her, "Am I to neglect my own talent, in order to serve you as a companion on your journies [sic]? Have you allowed your talent to lie useless, or ought you to do so, because I am chained to the paper and to the piano?"

When they were together, if Robert sat at his piano and composed, it was impossible for Clara to practice or compose on *her* piano. Robert needed quiet in order to do his work. This was a time when his creativity was at a peak, and he worked feverishly, often for hours without a break. Clara wrote in the marriage journal, "If only the room partitions were not so thin! I fear my piano playing will deteriorate altogether."

A month after Clara's return from Copenhagen, she confided her frustration to her diary, "I am getting behind with my playing, which always happens when Robert composes."

Yet Clara's desire to compose could not be dampened. Despite the little time she had to sit at the piano, she continued to write new music. From 1840 to 1842, Clara composed *Sechs Lieder mit Begleitung des Pianoforte (Six Songs with Piano Accompaniment*) based on poems by Heinrich Heine, Emanuel Geibel, and Friedrich Ruckert, three of the most famous German poets of the time. She dedicated them to Queen Caroline Amalie of Denmark. They were published in 1843 by the Leipzig publishing company Breitkopf & Hartel.

A few months after Clara's return home, her father did an about-face: he wanted to reestablish his relationship with his daughter and son-in-law. Wieck invited them to come to Dresden to visit him and asked them to bring his granddaughter. If they couldn't come to Dresden, he said, he'd come to Leipzig to see them. Clara continued to win applause as her career moved ahead, and Robert had composed several symphonies, which his father-in-law considered the work of a real composer.

Clara was excited by her father's offer of reconciliation. She wrote to him, "I should have been delighted to accept your kind invitation at once, but you know one cannot always get away, and the time of year is too rough for baby now. As soon as it grows warmer again I shall bring her over, and you will be delighted with her."

She invited him to visit her, which he did early in February 1843. Later, she traveled to Dresden and visited him and Clementine. "Father is now heart and soul for Robert's compositions," she reported in mid-February, after her visit to Dresden for a private performance of Schumann's music and to see her father. She was pleased that her father now appreciated her husband's music.

Clara's happiness was now complete. She was reunited with her father, married to the man she loved, and had a young daughter. And, on April 25, 1843, she gave birth to a second daughter, Elise.

Robert was equally happy. Clara was once more at home, resting from her tour, and again the wife and mother that he loved. After his frenzied period of composing while she was away, Robert became depressed for a short time. He would suffer from periods of depression for the next few years. He was glad that Clara was at home to take care of him.

During the months when Clara was in Leipzig, she continued to perform locally. She gave several concerts at the *Gewandhaus* and, after Elise's birth, ventured a little farther away to give a few concerts in nearby Dresden. She traveled to Dresden by a new railroad that connected the two cities.

But even short separations caused Robert to write pathetically about how he needed and missed her. "There is a strange silence in the house, but it seems to me that your dear spirit is everywhere. . . . I was very sorry for the poor papa; he was depressed. Marie is well; when she hears the word 'Mama' she waves her hand sadly as if she knew you were gone."

While at home Clara and her husband studied the work of other musicians and played music together. Robert began to compose feverishly again.

Everything seemed to go well for the Schumanns in the spring of 1843. There was a second daughter in the house and Robert began to compose his cantata, *Das Paradies und die Peri* (*Paradise and the Fairy*), a musical work for solo voice, chorus, and orchestra. He also accepted a teaching position at the Leipzig Conservatory. Although Clara had earned a good amount of money from her recent concert tour, expenses had to be paid and money was still scarce in the Schumann household.

By the end of 1843 Robert completed *Peri*. He planned to conduct its rehearsals and the first performance. The opera took up Clara's time, too. She took part in arranging the portion of the musical score that was for voices and the piano and acted

Robert and Clara Schumann in 1847 by Eduard Kaiser
(Courtesy of Lebrecht Music and Arts Photo Library/Alamy)

as an intermediary between her husband and the musicians. Robert was not a good communicator and, as a result, rehearsals were less than professionally conducted. When the opera premiered in December, it was not well received by critics or the audience, neither of which found it interesting.

In January 1844 Clara and Robert embarked on a concert tour to Russia, where she planned to perform in St. Petersburg and Moscow. She had looked forward to the trip since the first year of her marriage but, for various reasons, the tour had been postponed several times. Robert agreed to accompany his wife because he was tired, having worked hard during the previous year.

Their first stop was in Schneeberg, where Robert's brother and his wife lived. The couple had agreed to care for Marie and Elise while their parents were in Russia. Clara and Robert then traveled over the frozen northern landscape by coach and sled and stopped overnight at inns along the way. Clara performed in various towns and cities in order to earn money to continue their journey to St. Petersburg and Moscow.

Clara withstood the cold and ice of the northern winter much better than her husband. She found the icy air bracing and exhilarating, but Robert became ill with a cold and fever. He felt weak and dizzy. At one point, he could not see and thought he was going blind.

The Schumanns arrived in St. Petersburg in early March. While Robert rested in their hotel room, Clara went sightseeing, met with musicians, and spoke with wealthy people who could help advance her career. She practiced the piano and gave several concerts.

Clara didn't notice that her husband's periods of depression were becoming more frequent and of longer duration. But others noticed his odd behavior. A man who was present at a soiree that the Schumanns attended, and where Clara played the piano, described the couple: "Schumann was, as usual, silent and withdrawn the whole evening. . . . Schumann sat mostly in a corner near the piano . . . with a sunken head, his hair was hanging in his face."

Clara gave a few concerts in St. Petersburg and was invited by the king and queen to play at the Winter Palace. At each concert she included some of Robert's compositions in the program. She was made an honorary member of the St. Petersburg Philharmonic Society.

In April, Clara and Robert went to Moscow, where Clara gave her scheduled concerts. She played some of her husband's pieces there, too.

The tour was a great success and earned Clara a significant amount of money. The Schumanns then returned home to Leipzig. It was difficult for Clara to adjust to being a housewife and mother after she had received such thunderous applause and praise for her performances, but she did it without complaint because it was expected of her as a woman.

That summer Clara joined her husband on the faculty of the Leipzig Conservatory, but their teaching jobs did not last long. Robert's health quickly became worse and it was obvious that he suffered from a nervous disorder. He was so weak that he could barely walk. He could not sleep, and he cried without reason.

Clara took Robert to the mountains, where she hoped that the clearer air would restore his health. When he did not improve, they made plans to go to Dresden for a while. They thought the air in Dresden was cleaner than in Leipzig and hoped the change would help Robert.

By this time the Schumanns expected their third child. Clara canceled a scheduled concert tour and took her husband to Dresden instead. In addition to the cleaner air, she thought the hills and slower pace of Dresden would be beneficial for him.

But Robert's health did not get better while they were in Dresden, either. Clara wrote in the marriage journal, "Robert didn't sleep at night, his imagination created the most frightening pictures, in the morning I usually found him bathed in tears, he gave up completely."

Yet the Schumanns decided to move permanently to Dresden. Clara wrote to her father, who said he knew of a vacant apartment they could rent. Wieck thought it could be ready for them by mid-December, if they wanted to come to Dresden quickly.

Clara agreed to rent the apartment, but she had a few concert engagements in Leipzig to fulfill before moving to Dresden. After two farewell concerts at the *Gewandhaus*, Clara and her husband packed up their household and left Leipzig, the city of Clara's birth.

A Time of Strife

On December 13, 1844, Clara and Robert Schumann moved their family to Dresden, an industrial city about seventy miles from Leipzig. They moved into an apartment that Clara's father had found for them on the ground floor of *Waisenhausstrasser* (Waisenhaus Street). On March 11, 1845, three months after they moved in, a third daughter, Julie, was born.

Clara and Robert began to study counterpoint, which is two or more melodies played at the same time. Clara was very pleased with this, since it gave her "great pleasure, for I saw—what I had never thought to see—a fugue of my own, and then several others, for we continue our studies regularly every day." A fugue is a form of imitative counterpoint where the melodies are played one after the other. Clara's fugues were published as *Drei Praeludein und Fugen fur das Pianoforte* (*Three Preludes and Fugues for the Piano*). Clara later surprised her husband with a printed copy of it on her birthday on September 13, 1845.

That spring Clara began to compose a Trio in G Minor for violin, cello, and piano, which she finished in September. It was her most ambitious work and would later be considered her best. During the next half-century, many musical groups played Clara's Trio. Robert and their friend Felix Mendelssohn, the renowned composer and orchestra conductor, were among those who respected this composition, but Clara considered it merely "effeminate and sentimental." Although she was initially pleased with her own compositions, Clara minimized her value as a composer throughout her life.

In June, Clara began to plan concerts she would give the following winter. She wrote in her diary, "Robert has added a beautiful last movement to his *Phantasie* in *A* minor for piano and orchestra, so that it has now become a concerto, which I mean to play next winter."

Since they now lived in the same city, Clara and her father saw each other from time to time. Although the relationship between the two improved somewhat, it remained strained. As if to taunt Clara, her father told her that he was grooming a new pupil for stardom: Clara's thirteen-year-old half-sister, Marie Wieck.

Clara did not think that Marie was particularly talented. She wrote in her diary, "She lacks spirit, and her playing strikes me as mechanical and joyless . . . what worries me about Marie is her technical deficiency. One must consider that the public expects more of child performers than in my day . . . . She [Marie] plays well but not excellently."

The critics agreed. When Marie and another of their father's pupils made their professional debuts, critics wrote negatively of the girls' performance and criticized Wieck, their teacher. Clara, who attended the performance, saw how nervous and worried her father was and felt pity for him.

During the first years after the Schumanns moved to Dresden, Clara had given fewer concerts than before, concentrating mainly on her husband's needs, her home, and her growing family. She gave piano lessons to supplement the family's income. Her concerts were local and were mainly designed to introduce her husband's works to audiences.

Composer and conductor Felix Mendelssohn
(Courtesy of the Library of Congress)

The center of the city of Leipzig *(Courtesy of the Library of Congress)*

The following year saw the birth of a son, Emil, on February 8, 1846. From birth he was sickly and very small in size. Soon after Emil was born, Clara accepted an invitation to the Leipzig *Gewandhaus* to premiere Robert's *Concerto in A-Minor.* She felt it would be good for Robert to have this work, which she considered his best composition, performed before an audience. She went to Leipzig and performed it there to favorable reviews.

In March both Clara and Robert attended a party at which Felix Mendelssohn was asked to play a Beethoven sonata (a musical form for one or more instruments). Mendelssohn told his host that he would only play the sonata if Clara would play the last movement. This was a public confirmation of how highly the famous composer and orchestra conductor respected Clara as a performer.

Clara thought he was just being polite. Reluctant to play, for fear she would perform poorly, she explained to the partygoers that she hadn't touched a piano in seven weeks. But when Mendelssohn got up from the piano before the piece was finished, Clara felt obligated to take his place and complete the sonata. It would have been impolite for her not to play. "He forced me to play it, and although the fright made me shake all over, it went fairly well," she wrote afterward.

The next month the Schumanns moved to a new apartment, on the first floor of a building at 20 *Reitbahnstrasse* (Reitbahn Street).

There, Robert underwent a burst of creativity and had renewed energy to compose. He worked without rest, although his doctors recommended that he not work so hard. Soon Robert began to hear ringing in his ears, and doctors told Clara to take her husband on a vacation so that he would be forced to rest.

Clara rented a small house in Maxen, a health resort, where one of its windows looked out over a mental institution not far away. Robert became upset when he saw the building and insisted that they not stay in Maxen. As a result, in July 1846 the family traveled to Norderney, an island in the North Sea. But soon, a mental institution would again figure prominently in the lives of both Clara and her husband.

The Schumanns went from Maxen to Hamburg by railroad and from Hamburg to Norderney by ship. They spent the summer in Norderney, where the salt air seemed to improve Robert's health. The family returned to Dresden at the end of August and Robert resumed a frantic pace of composing and writing.

In October Clara began to rehearse her Trio in G Minor for violin, cello, and piano. She was, at first, pleased with her composition. Her diary says, "There is nothing greater than the joy of composing something oneself, and then listening to it. There are some pretty passages in the trio and I think it is fairly successful as far as form goes." But as she continued to play, she thought it less important and creative because it had been composed by a woman. When she compared it with a piano quartet her husband had composed, she liked her Trio even less.

Later that year Clara left Dresden on a bitterly cold morning to begin a concert tour to Vienna. She went with Robert and their two eldest daughters, Marie and Elise. As before, the younger children were left at home in the care of servants. Along the way, as was customary, concerts were hastily set up so that Clara could earn enough to continue the trip.

The tour proved a keen disappointment for both Clara and Robert. Clara's Vienna concerts were not well-attended. Concert-goers had forgotten the brilliant piano virtuosa who had performed there nine years earlier. As a result the concert halls were mostly empty. The critics were not enthusiastic, either. They thought that both Clara and the pieces she chose to play were too serious, although they wrote favorably about her playing. They were even less enthusiastic about Robert's compositions, which she included in all her performances.

On the evening following their departure from Vienna, Clara performed in a theater in Brunn. The cold weather still lingered. Clara wrote, "I shall never forget this evening, my fingers kept growing stiff while I played, my teeth chattered, in fact it was indescribable. After each piece I thought, 'I cannot go on any more.'" As cold as the evening was, the theater was crowded and the audience was appreciative.

The Schumanns stopped in Prague next, as they made their way toward Dresden and home. As in Vienna, Clara played some of her husband's compositions during her performances in Prague. Robert conducted his *Concerto in A-Minor* there and Clara happily noted in her diary that it was well-received by the audience, who called Robert back onstage to take another bow when he finished. When he hesitated, Clara pushed her husband out onto the stage to thunderous applause.

The Schumanns and their daughters arrived in Dresden on February 4, 1847, where they were glad to be reunited with the youngest children. After resting at home for a few days Clara and Robert set out once again, leaving all their children at home. They went to Berlin for the first performances of Robert's *Das Paradies und die Peri* at the Berlin *Singakademie*, a famous music school.

While Robert conducted the rehearsals, Clara played the piano. At the premiere performance of *Peri* on February 17, the king of Berlin was in attendance and the hall was quite full. The performance went well and the newspapers reviewed it favorably.

Within a few days of their arrival in Berlin, Clara began to feel at home and comfortable there. She visited with her mother, who still lived there. "It was so pleasant in Berlin to have my Mother, who sympathized with everything, who rejoiced with me, and at the same time was so fond of Robert that she could well understand my love for him." She was also able to talk frankly with her mother about personal things she could not tell her husband or her children.

She made many new friends in Berlin and enjoyed soirees and musical afternoons in the homes of wealthy people who were interested in music. The king and princess of Prussia attended one of those social engagements.

Berlin, Germany, in the mid-1800s

Clara was also invited to visit at the homes of members of Felix Mendelssohn's family and felt most comfortable on those occasions. One afternoon, at a luncheon at the home of Mendelssohn's brother-in-law, Clara met the composer's sister, Fanny Hensel, herself a composer and pianist. Clara wrote, "I have taken a great fancy to Madame Hensel and feel especially attracted to her in regard to music . . . and her conversation is always interesting, only one has to accustom oneself to her rather brusque manner."

She admired Fanny Hensel's ability as a pianist, but not as a composer. Clara still considered compositions written by women inferior to those written by men. She wrote "A woman must not wish to compose—there never was one able to do it."

By this time Clara and Robert had been away from Dresden for a month, and they missed their children and their home. On March 24, immediately after Clara's final concert, the Schumanns left Berlin. They stopped in Leipzig the next day for a brief visit with Felix Mendelssohn. It was the last time they would see their friend. He died a short time later, six months after the death of his sister Fanny.

They were reunited with their children in Dresden on March 25. All of the children were well except for Emil, their youngest. Yet Clara had mixed feelings about being home. "Happy as I was to be with the children again, yet the sudden quiet, after so active a life, was unpleasant for the first few days, but I soon became used to it."

Felix Mendelssohn's sister, Fanny, also a pianist and composer
(Courtesy of Bildarchiv Preussischer/ Art Resource, NY)

Clara set to work writing the piano arrangement for her husband's most recent symphony. This helped her get used to being at home again and taking care of husband, home, and children. In May she began to compose the first movement of a concertino in E minor, which she wanted to present to Robert as a birthday present the following month.

But she was acutely aware that she had not made any friends in the four years since moving to Dresden. She had her father and stepmother nearby, but her relationship with her father was still strained, and she and Clementine, her step-mother, never got along well. Clara wanted to leave Dresden, perhaps for Berlin, where she at least had her mother. But there was as yet no real reason to go.

Clara was pregnant again, and was concerned that giving birth to so many children would interfere with her career as a concert performer and, as a result, there would be less money coming into the Schumann household. "And what will become of my own work?" she asked in her diary. "I do not know whether things can always go on like this."

Then she tried to look at the bright side of the situation. "But Robert says: 'Children are blessings,' and he is right for there is no happiness without children, and therefore I have determined to face the difficult time that is coming, with as cheery a spirit as possible. Whether I shall always be able to do so or not, I do not know."

Tragedy struck on June 22, when sixteen-month-old Emil died. But Clara had little time to grieve. In July she and Robert left Dresden to attend a music festival in Robert's honor in Zwickau, where he had been born. He conducted his C Major Symphony there on July 10.

Clara performed during the festival as well. On the Sunday following the concert, everyone in Zwickau assembled in the town hall. When Clara and Robert arrived there, a flourish of trumpets greeted them. Loud cheers came from the crowd and everyone wanted to shake Robert's hand. He was truly the hometown hero, and Clara was as proud of his talent as was everyone else in Zwickau.

On January 20, 1848, another son, Ludwig, was born. Clara spent the early months of the year at home taking care of her house and children. She performed on both organ and piano at the *Caecilieverein* (Society of St. Cecilia), a choral society that Robert had founded. It was her first performance in many months. She also played a concerto of her husband's at the *Gewandhaus*. Both appearances were greeted with enthusiastic and lengthy applause. Meanwhile Robert began work on his new composition, *Genoveva*.

That summer Clara kept herself busy at home. Besides her household and family duties, she worked on the piano score of *Genoveva*, took on additional students, and occasionally acted as her husband's assistant at the choral society. But she had little time to practice on the piano or to compose. As always, when Robert composed he needed quiet in the house. Clara complained to her diary, "My piano playing is falling behind. This always happens when Robert is composing. There is not even one little hour in the whole day for myself! If only I don't fall too far behind. . . . I can't do anything with my composing."

At the beginning of May 1849, rebels revolted against the government and there was fighting in the streets of Dresden. The rebels went door-to-door in the city to recruit men to fight with them. They came to the Schumann residence in an attempt to convince Robert to join them. Clara, now seven months pregnant with their sixth child, spoke to the rebel soldiers, while her husband hid himself in the house. She made excuses for why he was not available.

Six of the eight Schumann children. From left to right: Ludwig,
Marie with Felix, Elise standing, Ferdinand, and Eugenie

When the soldiers left, Clara, Robert, and their daughter, Marie, packed a few things and fled. They went by train to Mugeln, eight miles outside of Dresden. Then they walked to a nearby village. They left their two younger daughters, Elise and Julie, and the baby, Ludwig, at home with the servants.

Clara was nervous about leaving her children behind in Dresden, but she knew that it would not be safe there for Robert. Two days later, with a woman to accompany her, Clara returned to Dresden on foot. She walked past armed soldiers, who did not stop her. Finally, Clara reached her home at 35 *Waisenhausstrasser* at night and found her children peacefully asleep in their beds. She woke them, packed some belongings, and led them out of the city to safety.

They returned to Dresden a few days after Robert's birthday in June. On July 16 another son, Ferdinand, was born.

On Clara's birthday in September, Robert surprised her with a *Geburtstagsmarsch* (*Birthday March*) that he had written especially for her. To celebrate the occasion, he and their daughter Marie played it as a duet for Clara.

Two months later Robert was asked to become the musical director of the Dusseldorf Orchestra and Chorus. The current director was about to retire and, because he was a friend of both Clara's and Robert's, he recommended that the position be offered to Robert. If Robert accepted the position, it would mean a move for the entire family to Dusseldorf, seventy miles west of Dresden.

The musical community of Dresden begged the Schumanns to stay. The musical community of Dusseldorf urged them to relocate there. "We live in a state of fatal indecision," Clara wrote in January 1850.

Clara was in favor of moving to Dusseldorf. She had no friends in Dresden and had never been completely happy there. In addition, there would be advantages to the move for Robert. As musical director, he would have sole responsibility for selecting the compositions the orchestra would perform. He would be required to prepare and conduct fourteen concerts each year. He would also be in charge of a 130-member choral society. Clara felt that the salary of 700 thalers Robert was offered was an acceptable amount that would go a long way toward paying the household bills.

Robert accepted the position, but before he and Clara could leave Dresden, both had to fulfill several concert engagements. At the end of August Robert's choral society in Dresden gave a farewell dinner for the Schumanns. On September 1, 1850, they left Dresden behind and moved to Dusseldorf.

CHAPTER 6

Dark Clouds Gather

When her husband accepted the position as musical director of the Dusseldorf Orchestra and Chorus, Clara Schumann packed up her household and moved with him, their children, and their servants to Dusseldorf.

They found a house for rent on *Grabenstrasse* (Graben Street) in a lower-class neighborhood. With such a large family and little income, their choices were limited. The house was on a noisy street, which was not ideal for the Schumanns, who needed quiet in order to compose and to play their music. Clara was unhappy with the situation and with her neighbors. She was used to being in the company of nobility and royalty. She noted in her diary, "I absolutely can't get used to the lower classes here, people for the most part coarse, cocky, and pretentious; they consider themselves our equals, not even saying good-day." Despite Clara's dissatisfaction, the Schumanns moved in.

Because she had no friends in Dresden and her relationship with her father and stepmother had not improved, Clara was happy nevertheless about the move to Dusseldorf. She considered it a good opportunity for her husband to advance his career. Her own reputation as a talented pianist followed her to Dusseldorf, too. Besides managing her household and family, Clara composed, performed locally, and taught students who came from all parts of Germany to study piano with her.

Unfortunately, it soon became obvious to the men who hired him that Robert was not the right person for the position of musical director. He was often depressed and did not communicate well with his musicians and singers. As a result, rehearsals went badly. Performers did not show up on time or take rehearsals seriously. Clara had to act as an intermediary between the orchestra and chorus and her husband, just as she had done when he rehearsed his opera, *Das Paradies un die Peri.*

She occasionally performed as pianist with the orchestra under Robert's direction. The first concert in which she participated was on October 24, 1851. Among the compositions on the program, the first one Robert conducted was Felix Mendelssohn's *Concerto in G-Minor.* Clara played the piano solo parts from memory, something her father had taught her because it would set her apart from other pianists. The audience was astounded, since most German pianists of the time still looked at the music while they played. Her performance was greeted with loud applause.

Clara was surprised and pleased that her memory had not failed her. But in her diary, she revealed her hesitation to place too much emphasis on it. She wrote, "Could this mean a return of youth's freshness and power? I don't think so, despite this evening's good result. The audacity required for memory playing is, after all, a concomittant [sic] [accompaniment] of youth."

At a reception afterward, Ferdinand Hiller, a composer and conductor who had attended the concert, proposed a toast to Clara. Robert's contribution to the success of the concert was ignored. Both Clara and Robert were angry and disappointed that only Clara was honored with the toast.

Yet Clara could not admit that her husband was not suited for the job as musical director. She made excuses for his shortcomings and felt that others did not appreciate him. She blamed the musicians and singers for a lack of professionalism. She also thought the Dusseldorf audiences less sophisticated than those in Leipzig and Dresden, and would have liked to leave Dusseldorf for a place where Robert's talents would be appreciated. But they had no other place to go. They had to make the best of their situation.

Meanwhile Robert's mental problems deepened. He became more and more depressed and found it hard to sleep. He barely spoke to the musicians and members of the chorus. Clara began to take over more of his day-to-day responsibilities, playing the piano at rehearsals of both the orchestra and the chorus. This was unusual for a pianist of Clara's star power. Concert pianists would usually consider it beneath them to play at rehearsals. But Clara loved her husband and he needed her help, so she did whatever was needed.

Robert was grateful for his wife's help, but his pride was hurt as well. He took out his frustrations on Clara and criticized her playing. He became angry one day while she was playing his *Quintet in E-flat Major* at a chorus rehearsal. He removed her from her position as rehearsal pianist and replaced her with his assistant, Julius Tausch. Clara was offended that her husband would treat her so unfeelingly.

As a child Clara had looked to her father for approval of her musical talents. She considered his continued approval proof that he loved her. Once she married she shifted her desire for approval to Robert. If he approved of her, she reasoned, he must surely love her. But now, she mistakenly thought that he was disappointed in her. Perhaps he no longer loved her. She wrote in her diary, "If I did not have to use my playing to earn some money, I would absolutely not play another note in public, for what good is it to me to earn the applause of the audience if I cannot satisfy him?"

On December 1, 1851, another daughter, Eugenie, was born. Soon after the birth Clara gave a few concerts locally. But because she now had six young children, she could not make long tours as she had in the past. She performed at the *Gewandhaus* in Leipzig, in Dusseldorf, and in the nearby cities of Bonn, Cologne, and Krefeld. In March 1852 Clara and Robert Schumann were invited to Leipzig for Schumann Week, a music festival that honored them both.

Despite these happy occurrences, Robert's career as a musical director continued to fall apart. The rehearsals constantly went poorly. At one chorus rehearsal in March 1852, a singer was so undisciplined that Clara became angry. She wrote, "There is nothing I would like better than for Robert to withdraw entirely from the Choral Society, for the position is not worthy of a man of his stature." To Clara, Robert Schumann was a genius who should not have to deal with the trivialities of life, such as earning a living.

By then it had become even more obvious to the directors of the Dusseldorf Orchestra and Chorus that Robert wasn't fit as musical director. The music journals began to write unfavorable comments about his abilities and about the unsuccessful concert season. It was obvious to everyone except Clara that Robert should resign. Instead, Clara continued to blame the members of the orchestra and chorus for a lack of professionalism, and the audiences for a lack of understanding of Robert's genius, as reasons for the poorly received concert season.

In 1852 Robert's mental state became even worse. He was more withdrawn than ever and hardly spoke to anyone, including Clara. When he did speak to her, he seemed short-tempered and angry. He became more and more critical of how she played the piano. Clara refused to acknowledge that there was anything more seriously wrong than that her husband was overworked—he continued to compose during this time—and directed musicians who did not take their work seriously.

In May 1853 Clara and her husband attended the Lower Rhine Music Festival, where Clara's performances were greeted with unrestrained applause. Her husband's mental condition had improved enough that he conducted one of the concerts there. At the festival they met Joseph Joachim, a violinist with whom Clara would develop a long and happy musical relationship.

By September Robert seemed to have recovered his good health. He was no longer so withdrawn and he began to compose feverishly again.

On September 30, 1853, a young composer named Johannes Brahms came to the door of the Schumann house.

Joseph Joachim

He said that the Schumanns' friend Joachim had suggested that he come to see them. He asked whether he could play one of his compositions for them. Twelve-year-old Marie, the Schumanns' oldest daughter, later described Brahms and that first meeting. "One day—it was in the year 1853—the bell rang toward noon. I ran out, as children do, and opened the door. There I saw a very young man, handsome as a picture, with long blond hair." Brahms asked to speak to Marie's father. She told him her parents were not at home, that they always go out at noon. When he asked when Robert would be at home, Marie told him to come back the next day at eleven o'clock.

When Brahms returned the following morning, the Schumanns agreed to listen to his music. They were so impressed with his fresh, bold style that they invited him to return time and time again to their home. Robert even helped Brahms get his first works published. Clara wrote her initial impressions of Brahms in her diary: "It is really moving to see him sitting at the piano, with his interesting young face, which becomes transfigured when he plays, his beautiful hands . . . and in addition those remarkable compositions . . . . He has a great future before him."

Brahms came to visit the Schumanns every day for the entire month of October. Clara, her husband, and Brahms spent each day talking, walking, and playing music together. In November Brahms returned to his home in Hamburg, Germany.

Early in November two representatives of the executive committee of the Dusseldorf Orchestra and Chorus came to the Schumann home to speak with Clara. They told her that in the future her husband would only conduct works that he had composed. Julius Tausch, Robert's assistant, would conduct all other pieces.

Johannes Brahms
(Courtesy of Pictorial Press Ltd /Alamy)

Clara became angry and refused to relay the message to her husband. But she wrote about it in her diary, where Robert was sure to see it. "What a shameful plot and an affront [insult] to Robert, for it would force him, in essence, to resign his position; I told all this to the gentlemen without even consulting with Robert," she concluded.

Robert responded that he considered the change in his responsibilities a violation of his contract. He and Clara chose not to attend a concert the following evening, where he was to conduct. The executive committee saw that as a breach of contract and relieved him of all responsibilities. They asked Julius Tausch to conduct the rest of the concerts that year and to become musical director the following year. What to do about the rest of Robert's contract, which had another year to run, would take more time to resolve.

Again Clara thought about leaving Dusseldorf, but she was a realist. She knew that her husband needed to keep his job as long as possible so that they could pay their bills. As she wrote in her diary, "With 6 children one can't just lift anchor and steer into the unknown."

Two weeks later Clara and Robert left Dusseldorf for a three-week concert tour in Holland. While there Clara gave ten concerts. At each she played at least one of Robert's compositions, and both she and her husband received praise and applause.

While they were on tour, discussions went on in Dusseldorf to determine whether Robert had broken his contract and what to do about it. Because the Dusseldorf Orchestra and Chorus was financed by the city of Dusseldorf, the mayor of the city was involved in the discussions. Given Robert's deteriorating mental condition and the reputation of both Schumanns, the mayor insisted that he be paid his full salary in 1854 regardless of whether or not he conducted any more concerts. Clara would be grateful for the mayor's generosity as the events of the next year began to unfold.

Busy as she was with caring for her family, helping her husband, and performing, Clara continued to compose during 1853. She wrote *Variationen fur das Pianoforte uber ein Thema von Robert Schumann* (*Variations for the Piano on a Theme by Robert Schumann*), *Drei Romanzen fur Pianoforte* (*Three Romances for the Piano*), *Drei Romanzen fur Pianoforte und Violine* (*Three Romances for Piano and Violin*), and *Zechs Leider aus Jucunde* (*Six Songs from Jucunde*).

By Christmas 1853 Clara was pregnant again and, as a result, gave up all thoughts of Robert leaving his position. They would just have to make the best of it even though she still insisted that her husband's genius was not being recognized in Dusseldorf.

The Schumanns left for a short tour to Hannover, Germany, the following month. They were welcomed by both Joachim and Brahms. There, Robert continued to be talkative and cheerful.

But by the time they returned to Dusseldorf in February, Robert's health problems were back. Clara could no longer close her eyes to her husband's mental condition. She had to admit that something was terribly wrong with him, finally seeing what had long been obvious to others who knew Robert. He was having a nervous breakdown.

He had stopped composing and spoke more frequently about hearing music when no music was being played. A violinist in the Dusseldorf Orchestra described what happened while he and Robert sat together in a restaurant. "Even as we were sitting [in the restaurant], his inner concert began and he was forced to stop reading his newspaper!" Schumann's headaches became worse and he couldn't sleep again.

Soon the music Robert heard in his head became less harmonious. He began to hear discordant, or unmusical, sounds and see demons lurking in the corners of the room.

The pregnant Clara became alarmed at her husband's odd behavior. She insisted that he be seen by a doctor. Afraid that he might hurt himself or someone else, Clara sat by his bedside at night and watched him carefully.

Near the end of February 1854 Robert insisted that he be placed in an institution for insane people. He admitted that he could not control his mind. He, too, feared that he might harm himself or his family. Doctors were summoned and Clara was no longer permitted to sit with him for fear he

would hurt her or their unborn child. Marie was asked to watch her father instead.

Clara wrote in her diary about how depressed Robert was: "When I merely touched him, he said, 'Ah, Clara, I am not wor-

The Endenich asylum where Robert was sent after his nervous breakdown

thy of your love.' *He* said that, he to whom I had always looked up with the greatest, deepest reverence [respect]."

On February 27, while Marie sat in a nearby room and Clara consulted with one of her husband's two doctors, Robert slipped out of the house alone. He walked to the nearby Rhine River and threw himself into the water. However, he was rescued before he could drown.

The doctors advised Clara to take her children and leave the house so that Robert would not become more nervous and upset. She agreed, and went to stay at the home of her friend Rosalie Leser, who lived nearby.

While they were gone Robert was brought back home and put to bed. He was guarded by his doctors' assistants for a few days until a place was ready for him at a mental hospital in Endenich, a short distance from Dusseldorf.

Convinced by the doctors that confinement at Endenich was the only way her husband would get better, Clara gave her permission. She was not permitted to see Robert before he went to Endenich. His doctors thought it could upset him too much to see her or their children. He was taken to the institution on March 4, 1854.

Little did Clara know that she would see her husband only one more time before his death.

CHAPTER 7

A Deepening Friendship

When Robert Schumann was taken to the mental institution at Endenich, Clara found it hard to believe that he was actually insane. She wrote in her diary, "Him, the magnificent Robert, in an institution!—how could I possibly tolerate this!" His doctors at Endenich told her not to visit him. Seeing her or their children would make Robert more upset and agitated, they said. It would speed his recovery if the family did not visit. Clara obeyed the doctors' request and stayed away.

But she knew that there would have to be other changes in her life. Even though the Dusseldorf Orchestra and Chorus had voted to continue Robert's salary through the end of his contract, she knew that income would only continue through the 1854 concert season. After that, it would be up to her to support herself and her family.

Many musicians and composers, on hearing that Robert had been sent to a mental institution, offered to play benefit concerts to raise money for Clara. Some even offered to give her money, but Clara refused all of their offers. She preferred to give her own concerts and earn money to support her family.

Clara began to think about the future. Besides her normal household expenses, she now had to pay for her husband's care at Endenich. She decided she would have to give additional concerts, even though it meant she had to arrange tours that would take her away from her home and children for long periods.

She began to give piano lessons again, both because she needed the income and because the lessons would keep her mind occupied so that she would not dwell on Robert's absence. She wrote, "It was a hard struggle, but on the one hand I felt as if nothing but the most strenuous activity could enable me to keep up, and on the other it is now doubly my duty to earn something."

Meanwhile, Johannes Brahms made daily visits to Clara and her children. He and Clara continued to play music together and to talk. Clara was grateful for his friendship. She wrote, "That good Brahms always shows himself a most sympathetic friend. He does not say much, but one can see in his face . . . how he grieves with me for the loved one [Robert] whom he so highly reveres. Besides, he is so kind in seizing every opportunity of cheering me by means of anything musical."

Clara missed her husband terribly and wrote to him regularly. She confided to her diary, "I feel very unwell, I cannot sleep at all by night, or if I do, I dream incessantly of Robert. . . . Last night I heard him sigh several times, so naturally that I had to look towards his bed to convince myself that it was not he."

This was the first time she and Robert had been separated during the thirteen years of their marriage. She was hopeful that he would recover his health and return home to her and their family in a short time.

In April Clara forced herself to concentrate on the pieces that she wanted to play in her upcoming concerts. She included a new composition that Brahms had written, *Trio in B Major* for piano, violin, and cello. She also played Robert's *Carnivale* and the *Requiem fur Mignon*. It was painful for her to play Robert's compositions, but Clara was determined to perform them.

By the end of the month Clara was not so certain that Robert's recovery would be speedy. She wrote in her diary, "I feel paralyzed, deprived of all will power; how shall I continue working under the blight of such hopelessness!"

An acquaintance from Leipzig visited Clara at her home in May. She found Clara "looking old and jaundiced [yellow], but not broken

Johannes Brahms
(Courtesy of World History Archive/Alamy)

or tearful." The friend said that Clara asked about their mutual friends and about her father, from whom Clara hadn't heard in a long time. There was no mention of Robert's illness until, suddenly, Clara burst into tears. She said that she had to believe that Robert would recover, because she could not live without him. She was also upset because her beloved husband had not yet asked to see her.

In the meantime, Brahms had rented rooms in a house near the Schumann home. He was grateful to Robert for his help in getting his first compositions published, and for the friendship that he and Clara had shown him. Brahms also felt protective toward Clara and wanted to do what he could to help during her husband's absence.

Clara had grown fond of Brahms, too. She was grateful for his continued friendship and for the help he offered. Some biographers speculate that Brahms had romantic feelings toward Clara. But although he wrote in some letters of his love for her, there is no evidence that Clara felt romantically toward him or that their relationship was ever more than that of valued friends who admired each other immensely.

On June 11, 1854, Clara gave birth to her eighth, and last, child. Clara named the boy Felix in honor of the Schumanns' friend Felix Mendelssohn. Soon after the birth, Clara began again to practice the piano in preparation for her first tour. She also made plans for the care of her children while she was away.

Clara's mother offered to take Julie, who was nine, to live with her in Berlin. Marie and Elise would remain at home to help the servants care for the older boys, who would go to school. Clara hired a nurse to care for two-and-a-half-year-old Eugenie and the baby, Felix. When Brahms offered to look after the children as well, Clara accepted, for he was fond of her children and they liked him.

Thus, at age thirty-five, Clara Schumann began again her career as a concert pianist. Many years had passed since she last had toured and Clara knew that audiences would not remember her. She also knew she would have to work twice as hard as before. She had no one to coach her this time, as her father and husband had done. But because of her character and her sense of responsibility for her family, she was able to resume performing in spite of having a large family and a husband who was ill.

She practiced tirelessly night and day to prepare herself for her concerts, noting in her diary,

> *I am haunted by music as never before; at night I cannot find sleep, and by day I am so absorbed by music that I lose track of all else, which is not like me.*

Marie and Elise gave a small concert to honor their mother on her birthday, September 13. Brahms helped them prepare for their performance, coaching and providing comments for improvement as they rehearsed secretly so it would be a surprise. Clara was appreciative of their efforts and proud of her daughters.

She also received a letter from Robert in which he seemed like his old self again. He wrote, "Oh, if I could see you and speak to you again, but the way is too far. So much I should like to know; how your life is going on; where you are living and if you still play as gloriously as formerly." Clara convinced herself that Robert's letter showed that he was recovering and would return home to her and their children. However, she was still not allowed to visit Robert for fear he would suffer a setback.

In mid-October, Clara left Dusseldorf accompanied by Brahms and Agnes Schonerstedt, who acted as her companion. She first went to Hannover, where she was received at court and played music with Joachim and other friends. She traveled on to Leipzig, where she performed music by Beethoven, Robert, and Brahms at the Leipzig *Gewandhaus*. Clara was well-received by audiences who, it seemed, had not forgotten her after all.

During the next three months Clara gave more than two dozen concerts in cities throughout Germany. While she toured, Brahms visited Robert and sent reports about his health to Clara.

Besides the travel and concert arrangements that she made in each city, Clara rehearsed and performed. She also ran her household and instructed her children through the letters she wrote to them. She earned enough money to pay her bills and to provide food, clothing, and education for the children. The nonstop effort drained Clara's strength and energy, although she still felt reenergized when she was on the stage.

Clara considered it her duty to play Robert's compositions for audiences. She also played pieces by Brahms. When Brahms urged her not to work so hard or her health would suffer, she told him, "I . . . believe that a quieter life would leave me too much time to brood on my sorrows." Her music enabled her to forget for short periods her sorrow about Robert's condition and to take pleasure in her work.

A sheet of Robert Schumann's handwritten notes
(Courtesy of iStockphoto.com)

In November she joined Brahms in Harburg, and the two friends then went to Hamburg together. There, Clara gave concerts and met Brahms' mother. When it was time for Clara to leave for Bremen, the next stop on her tour, she wrote of Mrs. Brahms, "It made me sad to say good-bye to the woman whose son has become so dear to me. I thought to myself, who knows how long this good mother may live? Perhaps I am appointed to be a mother to him in her place." Clara, who was fourteen years older than Brahms, felt maternal toward the young man.

In Berlin, where Clara gave a concert at the *Gewandhaus*, she visited the home of her friend Felix Mendelssohn's brother. Paul Mendelssohn had offered to lend her money when he heard that Robert had been taken to Endenich. Joachim came to Berlin, too, and he and Clara played music together at soirees in the homes of wealthy music lovers. They played Robert's music as well as pieces by Bach, Beethoven, and Felix Mendelssohn.

Clara returned home in time to spend Christmas with her family. Hoping that Robert would be home soon, she made holiday preparations and trimmed a tree for him. But only Brahms and her children spent Christmas with Clara. She was

(Courtesy of iStockphoto.com)

disappointed that her husband was not there, but her children were happy to see Brahms and all enjoyed the holiday together.

Just as Robert Schumann had become a member of the Wieck household years earlier, Johannes Brahms played a similar role in the lives of the Schumanns. Both men played games with the children of the house and enjoyed their company.

January 1855 found Clara on tour again, giving concerts in Germany and the Netherlands. On March 4, the first anniversary of Robert's removal to Endenich, Clara noted in her diary, "A year ago to-day [sic], Robert went to Endenich. I was very sad this morning." She returned to Germany to perform the following month and, in May 1855, performed at the music festival in Dusseldorf. That fall she again toured with violinist Joseph Joachim.

During this period, Clara received several letters from Robert, but as the months passed they became fewer and fewer. Finally, on May 5 Clara received the last letter she would ever get from her husband. On May 9 Clara and her children celebrated Brahms' twenty-second birthday in their home. Clara described the party, which included dancing: "He was very merry, and thoroughly enjoyed it so that I too seemed to grow younger, for he whirled me along with him and I have not spent so cheerful a day since Robert fell ill."

As summer approached Clara received an invitation to go to Detmold, Germany, and give piano lessons to Princess Friederike, sister of the reigning prince. Although Clara did not want to leave Dusseldorf, where both Brahms and Joachim were at the time, she felt she had to go. Besides giving piano lessons, she was able to give musical soirees at the palace in Detmold. She returned home on July 1. Three days later, without telling anyone, Clara traveled to Endenich in an attempt to visit Robert. Disappointed that doctors would not allow her to see him, she returned to Dusseldorf.

As in the past, Clara took refuge in her music, relearning old pieces and adding new ones to her repertoire. She played them all from memory, the way her father had taught her. She committed an impressive number of pieces to memory, including more of Robert's compositions, which featured prominently in her concerts. Since Robert could no longer introduce his works to audiences, Clara felt that was her responsibility. She also included Brahms' works.

In September the doctors sent word that Robert's health would never improve. They said he would have to remain at Endenich permanently. His mental condition had deteriorated so much that he no longer recognized Brahms, who visited him regularly. His speech was garbled and he would remain silent for long periods of time. Clara felt confused,

Joseph Joachim playing violin with Clara accompanying him on the piano

not knowing whether it would be better to have him home with her in his present condition or not at all.

That year, for her birthday, many of her friends gave Clara gifts of music. Brahms presented her with parts from his latest musical composition. Her eldest daughters played music for her in her honor. Still, Clara was sad that Robert could not be with her.

When the winter concert season began in October, Clara was on the road again, giving concerts in several German cities. While in Berlin she visited her mother. She also gave several concerts there with Joachim, playing the music of Bach, Beethoven, and Robert Schumann. Brahms arrived in Berlin the next month and he, Clara, and Joachim gave two concerts together. "We three belong together as artists, and I am very glad that for once we shall be able to appear together in public," she wrote. When Brahms left Berlin, Clara and Joachim went to Leipzig for their last concert of the year together early in December. She returned to Dusseldorf in time to celebrate Christmas 1855 with Brahms and her children.

It was a successful concert tour for Clara, but Robert's illness cast a cloud on an otherwise happy time. If only the doctors at Endenich would reverse their diagnosis and tell Clara that her husband would get well. It was not to be.

CHAPTER 8

Widowhood

The year 1856 saw Clara on tour again. This tour was extensive and she traveled farther than before—to Vienna, Budapest, and Prague.

Before leaving she arranged for the care of her children. Marie, fifteen, and Elise, thirteen, were enrolled in a Leipzig boarding school. Julie remained in Berlin with her grandmother. The four youngest children—Ludwig, Ferdinand, Eugenie, and Felix— were at home in Dusseldorf with Clara's housekeeper. Brahms lived in a separate apartment in the same building and helped with the care of the children at home.

In June Clara traveled to England, where she spent more than two months giving concerts. One concert featured Robert's *Das Paradies und die Peri* (*Paradise and the Fairy*), a cantata for solo voice, chorus, and orchestra. Queen Victoria of England was in the audience, which became preoccupied with their monarch. They pointed toward the queen and whispered among themselves rather than concentrate on the music. Clara, who was singing in the chorus at the time, was annoyed.

Later, at a soiree in a private home, the guests talked to each other while Clara played the piano. She was so angry with their lack of manners that she stopped playing. "I let my hands lie in my lap, and did not begin to play again until everyone was quiet. If more artists did that, they would be more respected," she wrote. She went on to say that the audience became silent and attentive and that the hostess later apologized to her.

She was just completing the tour when she received a telegram from one of Robert's doctors. His condition had worsened. Clara's diary entry reflects her ambivalent feelings: "What a thought, to see him, the most zealous of artists, mentally weakened, perhaps, or far more likely, prey to the most terrible melancholy? Do I want to have him *like this*?" On the other hand, wouldn't she want her husband back no matter what his physical and mental condition? Either way, she thought, the situation would be terrible. She went to the mental institution at Endenich as soon as she could, but again was denied a chance to see Robert. The doctors felt that his appearance would be too shocking for Clara.

Toward the end of July Clara returned to Endenich accompanied by Brahms. This time the doctors allowed her to see Robert, for they expected that he would die within a day or two. Clara spent July 27 and the following day visiting her husband. She wrote in her diary, "For weeks he had had nothing but wine and gelee [jelly]—today I gave it to him—and he took it with the happiest expression and in haste, licking the wine from my fingers—ah, he knew that it was I." It was the first time in more than two years that she saw Robert.

The next day Clara and Brahms left Endenich for a short time to meet Joachim at the railroad station. They were away for about an hour. When they returned to the institution, they learned that Robert had died. Clara wrote in her diary, "I stood at the body of my dearly loved husband and was calm; all my feelings were of thankfulness to God that he was finally free. . . . I placed some flowers on his brow—he has taken my love with him!"

The official cause of Robert's death was a nervous disorder made worse by overwork. Some biographers think that Robert may have contracted syphilis, a sexually transmitted disease, when he was a young man. They say that the medicine doctors gave him to cure the syphilis may have affected his brain and resulted in his mental problems. Others speculate that the syphilis remained in his body without any outward signs. Although untreated syphilis can result in mental problems and even death, there is no real evidence that he had the disease. Clara certainly never contracted it, despite bearing Robert eight children.

Two days later Clara buried her beloved husband in a churchyard in Bonn. Brahms and Joachim attended the service with Clara. She wanted only friends who knew and loved Robert to be there. "God give me strength to live without him . . . with his departure, all my happiness is over. A new life is beginning for me," she wrote after the service.

So began Clara Schumann's long widowhood.

Clara returned to Dusseldorf after the funeral. In a letter to Joachim she later confided that it was one of the most difficult periods of her life. "I had come there with husband and children, full of the fairest hopes, and now I was going forth alone; he was in his grave, and my friends were far away," she told her friend.

Emotionally drained as she was, Clara knew she had to prepare for the winter concert season that was about to begin. She arranged for her eldest sons, Ludwig and Ferdinand, who were eight and seven, respectively, to go to a boarding school in Herchenbach. She confided to her diary, "I felt terrible, but it is certainly in their best interests" to be sent away to school. Her two youngest children remained at home with her housekeeper.

In 1857 Clara moved her family to Berlin. She had sad memories of Dusseldorf, where she and Robert had lived

before his illness. Berlin, on the other hand, held no memories of Robert, and Clara could be closer to her mother.

Clara and Joachim performed together in both Dresden and Leipzig. From there, she traveled with a female companion to Munich in southern Germany. She was warmly received by the audience there.

But before she arrived in Munich, her left arm began to hurt. By the end of 1857 her arm gave her so much pain that she was forced to cancel a concert. She told Joachim about it. "Upon medical examination it turns out to be rheumatic

The Victoria Hotel in Berlin, circa the late 1800s
(Courtesy of the Library of Congress)

inflammation caused partly by over-work and partly by catching cold . . . . I have been unable to do anything, as the pain has been incessant, and it gives me no rest." A painful arm could end a pianist's career.

Fortunately, the first part of 1858 found Clara on tour again. She was able to give concerts in Switzerland and in Stuttgart, Germany. On the way back to Berlin, she stopped off to visit Ludwig and Ferdinand at their school and found both doing well. That summer Clara and all of her other children went on vacation together in Gottingen, a resort area where Clara rented rooms. In September the children returned to school and home, while Clara began another tour.

This time Marie accompanied her. Mother and daughter went to Dresden and Prague before they continued on to Vienna and Budapest. As in the past, Clara included Robert's music in her concerts and soirees.

Clara and Marie returned to Berlin in early April 1859 to spend Easter with the children and Brahms. Then she set out for a return trip to London with her half-sister, Marie Wieck. She met Joachim there and the two musicians performed together in several concerts.

That fall Clara changed the schools Ludwig and Ferdinand attended. Her concern for Ferdinand showed in a letter to a family friend: "I ask nothing more for him than a small room to sleep in and where he can also work on Sundays and evenings, and a simple but hearty diet; at noon he should regularly have as much meat as he wants, as he is growing frightfully fast." Although she could not visit them often, she was well aware of how the boys and their sisters were doing in their respective schools. Clara often sent letters of advice and instructions to her children.

She told her friend Emilie List how demanding her life was as a single mother of a large family. "Just think, having five children boarded out in three different places, and getting their wardrobe in order for the changing seasons," she confided. Her feelings and experiences were similar to those of today's working mothers.

Even her youngest children understood why their mother could not be at home with them. Eugenie wrote, "Wherever she might be, we were ever conscious of her loving care, her protecting hold over us, and that to us little ones, as well as to the elder sisters and brothers, she was the greatest thing we possessed in the world."

Clara's concert tour continued well into December, and it was after Christmas Day before she was able to return to Berlin to spend the remainder of the holiday with the children. Brahms and Joachim visited with the Schumanns for a short while early in January 1860. Then Clara set out again on a tour, taking her daughter Elise with her this time. After a month-long tour with performances in Germany and Holland, Clara and Elise returned to Berlin.

But Clara didn't stay home for long. After a short rest, she left for another tour. This time she went to Vienna for three performances, which sold out well in advance. Although the concerts brought Clara much satisfaction, they did not bring a great deal of money. She wrote to Joachim that she had finally decided to play the trio she had composed. "What do you say or think of such courage? It is the first time that I [will] have played it in public, and indeed I am only doing so now because I have been urged to it on all sides," she explained to her friend.

On the way home from Vienna, Clara made a detour to Leipzig for a concert and a visit with her father. She returned home to Berlin for a two-week rest and was off again to

Daguerreotype of Clara Schumann at her piano by Franz Hanfstaengl in 1860
(Courtesy of INTERFOTO/Alamy)

Hamburg, where Brahms convinced her to remain for several weeks before returning to Berlin on May 1. She promised Brahms, however, that she would return to Hamburg again to help him celebrate his birthday on May 7. During the summer, with the concert season over, Clara visited friends in Dusseldorf and Bonn and spent time with her children in the resort town of Kreuznach.

That summer and early fall, Brahms sent Clara some of his new compositions. She played them, liked them very much, and gave Brahms suggestions for improving them. Around this time, both Brahms and Joachim encouraged her to publish some of Robert's compositions. Brahms told her, "Schumann himself intended them to be printed and had fully prepared them." Clara took their suggestion to heart and in future years collected and published her husband's work.

In September Clara began to think again about her upcoming concert season. First she had to make certain her children were well provided for. She left Kreuznach after she brought her two youngest, Eugenie and Felix, to her friend Elisabeth Warner in Berlin. Warner had agreed to let them stay with her while Clara toured. She gave her daughter Julie into the care of another friend in Coblenz.

By the end of November, Clara found herself in Leipzig for a concert in which both Brahms and Joachim performed. Brahms conducted his second *Serenade*. The audience did not react as warmly to it as Clara did and she felt bad for her friend. Brahms and Joachim performed other compositions, which received more applause and a more positive reaction from the audience.

Clara continued touring through the end of 1860, playing concerts and soirees in various cities in Germany, some with Brahms and Joachim. That year, she was unable to spend

Christmas with her youngest children. She wrote to them, "On Christmas Eve when you are very happy, think of your Mamma, who would so love to be with you . . . . I kiss you in all motherly love and tenderness."

During 1861 Clara's success continued in Belgium and

Julie Schumann

Switzerland. By now Clara's concerts included many of Brahms' works as well as her husband's. By December Clara was back in Germany for concerts in Hamburg and Leipzig. This time, she was able to spend Christmas with her children and with Joachim. Brahms joined them soon afterward and spent the first few days of the new year with them.

After the children returned to school, Clara continued her tour of German cities. By the end of the month, her arm again ached so badly that it had to be placed in a sling when she was not performing. Yet she continued to play. In May she and Marie journeyed to Paris, where

Clara was determined to introduce Parisian audiences to the music of Brahms and Robert Schumann. She played Brahms' *Serenades* and his *Handel-Variations* (*Variations on a Theme by Handel*) and Robert's *Trio in D Minor* many times while she was in the French capital.

On her way home she stopped in Dresden to visit her father and his family. "I am so glad to be with my Father, he is in such good spirits and I am so fond of him that my heart always leaps for joy when I see him, although our character [sic] are not at all in harmony," she told her diary during the visit.

That summer Clara went to Kreuznach for a vacation with daughters Marie, Julie, and Eugenie. They spent a few days in Baden-Baden, a resort Clara had not visited before. There, she bought a small house to have a place of her own where she and the children could spend summer vacations. By September she was on the road to Holland, accompanied by Marie. Now, migraine headaches added to the constant discomfort of her aching arm, but she continued to rehearse and perform anyway.

The family spent the summer of 1863 at the house in Baden-Baden. Many friends came to visit and the house was filled with music.

In January 1864 Clara returned to Russia. As during her earlier trip there with Robert, she gave successful concerts along the way in order to finance the tour. She included Robert's compositions in her concerts, of course. She told Brahms, "It has given me great pleasure to find many warm admirers of Robert's everywhere, and I can truly say that Robert's works are amongst those with which I have the greatest success." In St. Petersburg Clara performed in the huge, 3,000-seat concert hall there. In April she played in Moscow before returning to Berlin. She spent the next few weeks performing in Dusseldorf and then retired to Baden-Baden to relax from the stress of months of traveling, organizing, rehearsing, and performing.

After another successful fall tour, in January 1865 Clara slipped and fell, injuring her right hand. She had to remain inactive for a few weeks while her hand healed. But once she could play the piano again, she resumed the tour, which took her to Zwickau, Germany, and Prague. By spring she, Marie, and her half-sister Marie Weick were in England again, before a now familiar return to the summer home in Baden-Baden.

For several years Clara was a popular concert draw in Germany, England, Scotland, Belgium, and Austria. She was usually accompanied by Marie, and monitored the progress of her other children from afar. Two of them—Ludwig and Julie— troubled her. Ludwig, who was now finished with school, was not settling down to his job with a bookseller; Clara worried about Julie's deteriorating health. From time to time Clara's injured right hand ached so badly that she was unable to play.

Despite her worries and discomfort, she continued to travel and perform. Each summer she returned to Baden-Baden to rest and give private piano and composition lessons to young women who wanted to learn music.

Although she had found success on her own, Clara's strength and determination would be tested even more in the years that followed.

CHAPTER 9

Family Troubles

As Clara toured, her children's troubles mounted. In late December 1867, word came to her that Julie, who was living with a friend of Clara's, was ill and had breathing problems. Clara could not go to her daughter because of scheduled concerts, but sent Marie to stay with Julie. Marie reported back that Julie was too ill to travel and could not return home. The next month Ludwig lost his job for failing to show up for work on time. Clara was able to find him another job with Breitkopf & Hartel, the Schumanns' publisher.

The news about Felix was far worse. Clara was told that he was showing the first signs of tuberculosis, a bacterial disease that weakens the lungs. As it turned out, Julie suffered from the same disease. Clara, touring, was devastated. In a letter to her friend Rosalie Leser, she wrote, "My heart bleeds as it has not since I went through all that with my poor Robert! I thought I had grown insensible through the years; still here I am, utterly overwhelmed!"

Felix had been staying with his grandmother in Berlin. In addition to his illness, he was not doing well in school.

He had no interest in his studies, but was obsessed with the idea of becoming a musician. Although Clara did not encourage her children to become performers due to the daunting schedule of traveling and giving concerts, she didn't discourage them, either. Among her children Felix was the one with real musical talent. But Clara knew what it would take for him to become a professional musician, especially since he would be known as the son of Robert Schumann.

She wrote to Felix about the difficulties he would face because of his name. "You can live up to that name only if, in music, you give evidence of extraordinary genius—and with it an enormous capacity for work." Good health was important for a performer, she knew, but Clara didn't want to discourage him entirely. She promised to send Felix's violin compositions to Joachim for his opinion.

Soon, Clara received news that Ludwig had lost his job again. His former employers advised Clara to send Ludwig to a mental institution since it was obvious that he was mentally ill. Just as she had refused to acknowledge Robert's deteriorating mental condition, Clara could not admit that Ludwig was mentally ill. She sent him to stay with his grandfather in Dresden.

As she returned home from Vienna, the last city on her tour, Clara stopped briefly in Dresden to see her family. She was appalled at how pale Ludwig had become. But after a brief visit with her father and son, Clara resumed her lengthy concert tour of Germany, Holland, and England.

The news from her daughter Julie got more complicated. Julie wanted to marry Vittorio Marmorito, an Italian count. He was a widower with two daughters. Julie had met Marmorito at a spa where she went for her health. Clara didn't approve of her daughter's engagement to an aristocrat who was not of her religion, spoke a different language, and moved in a world very different from Julie's. She confided to her diary, "I have told her [Julie] all my misgivings, though more to ease my own conscience, since love will not be thwarted; this I know from my personal experience." But remembering how her father had tried to interfere with her own marriage to Robert, Clara gave the couple her approval and they married on September 22, 1869.

In 1870 Clara finally accepted Ludwig's mental problems. She sent him to a clinic, which confirmed that he should be institutionalized. Clara told Rosalie Leser that the confirmation of Ludwig's illness "struck my heart like a frightful blow—it is a pain like no other." Clara sent Ludwig to a mental institution in Colditz.

In her diary, she admitted that the situation with Ludwig reminded her of Robert. She wrote, "I have not felt such pains since the misfortune with Robert. . . . The nights were often dreadful; for hours I would see the poor boy before me, looking at me with his good, honest eyes, which I never could resist."

While traveling to Baden-Baden in July Clara noticed that preparations were being made for war. She noted in her diary, "No-one is allowed to use the railway any more . . . if anyone wishes to leave they must go by the military roads, and traveling is very slow. . . . I have hidden all my valuables, and even some of the wine in the cellar." While she was worried that war was imminent, her children did not seem too concerned. Their lack of worry made Clara less anxious about the possibility that fighting would soon break out. However, on July 19, the Franco-Prussian War began when France declared war on Germany.

At the time Germany consisted of a group of separate independent states and was called Prussia. France, under emperor Napoleon III, was seeking to regain its lost influence in Europe. Napoleon feared the Prussian army, which had grown more powerful since 1866, when Prussia defeated Austria in the Austro-Prussian War. For his part, Prince Otto von Bismarck of Prussia wanted to eliminate France's influence in the German states entirely and unify those states into one country under Prussian control.

With the declaration of war the German states rallied to the support of their countrymen, sending soldiers to fight against their common enemy. Clara's son Ferdinand was called to serve in the German army. She shared the news with Rosalie Leser: "Just think, my poor boy has already been drafted and

beginning tomorrow he must undergo training for four to five weeks after which, if the emergency continues, he will be sent to the front. But one cannot stop to think of one's child at such a time as this, when all Germany is anxious for her sons." Her letter reflected the conflict she felt between worry over her own son and the worry of all mothers when their children go to war.

When the war ended in 1871 Bismarck had achieved his goal. France was defeated and the Prussian states were unified

The Battle of Reichshoffen, fought on August 6, 1870, during the Franco-Prussian War

The Battle of Mars-la-Tour, fought on August 16, 1870, in France during the Franco-Prussian War

into a single country called Germany under Kaiser Wilhelm I. The good news was that Ferdinand Schumann was discharged from the army. The bad news: by then, he had become addicted to the drug morphine, which had been given to him in the army to treat painful rheumatism.

In November 1871 Brahms spoke to Clara about an open position for a music teacher in the Berlin Conservatoire. He suggested that she apply, but Clara refused to consider it. She was a concert performer, not a piano teacher. But in December, while on tour in Frankfurt, Clara had her own attack of rheumatism in her arm. The pain was so severe that she could not play the piano for ten days. Only after the pain subsided could she resume her performances. Not being able to honor all her concert commitments meant a heavy financial loss for Clara.

The terrible pain in her arm recurred in April 1872 in London. As she was about to leave for home, she received a summons from Queen Victoria to give a concert at Buckingham Palace. Her arm hurt terribly. She'd been away from home for a long time. To make matters worse, her mother had died in March and Clara was unable to attend the funeral because of concert commitments. Clara desperately wanted to go home, but knew it was a great honor to be invited to play at the palace. She found the experience disappointing, since the queen didn't seem at all interested in the music. Her diary entry explained how insulted she was by the queen's poor manners: "When it was all over she did not utter a word of thanks. Never in my life has such a thing happened to me. This Queen is not going to see me under her roof again; of that I am sure! A dinner had been prepared for us in the anteroom where we left our coats! But I declined." Clara, a highly honored concert artist, was accustomed to receiving praise and applause whenever she performed. It was an insult to her to be expected to eat her dinner in the coat room.

Now Clara began to consider the teaching position that Brahms had mentioned. She wrote to the Berlin Conservatoire about what it would take for her to accept the position, including the option of taking a leave of absence from the music school whenever she needed to go on a concert tour or for summer vacations. She also asked to choose her students and to receive a salary of 4,000 thalers each year. The Conservatoire gave the position to someone else.

Clara headed home after the concert at Buckingham Palace in London. Despite the pain in her arm, she performed in Brussels, Belgium, on her way back to Germany. By early May she had reached Germany, where she gave a concert in Dusseldorf. Then she returned home to Berlin to plan a summer vacation in Baden-Baden with all her children.

Victoria, queen of Great Britain

Julie and her husband and family visited Clara in Baden-Baden in the summer of 1872. Seeing her, Clara realized that her daughter's illness could not be cured. It was the last time they saw each other. Julie died on November 10 while Clara was preparing to perform in Heidelberg. Clara received a telegram about her daughter's death, but it was too late for her to cancel the performance. She did not attend Julie's funeral.

She explained her apparent lack of emotion in a letter to a friend, writing, "I am calm because, since the first day I saw the dear child again in Baden [in the summer of 1872] I was convinced that she would not live much longer. Our first embrace was like a blow to my poor heart; the worry did not leave me for an instant and that may well account, alas, for my calmness now." Clara added that she felt she had lost Julie at the time of her daughter's marriage, anyway.

The following year Clara lost her father. Friedrich Wieck died on October 6, 1873, at the age of eighty-eight. Clara wrote in her diary, "I am deeply shaken, for with him goes the last link to my youth. I loved him intensely. . . . Even though we were not always in accord [agreement] this never lessened my love, since I was bound by lifelong gratitude." She recalled how her father had devoted years to teaching her and directing her career. She had forgiven Wieck's erratic behavior toward her and Robert before their marriage, and she mourned his death.

More distressing news about her children followed. Felix now found breathing so difficult that he could no longer walk to school.

Ferdinand worked for a Berlin bank after his release from the army. On August 13, 1873, he married Antonie Deutsch. As when Julie married, Clara was not happy. She thought it would be better for Ferdinand to wait until his career was established before he married. She wrote, "now, with one stroke, all these hopes are in vain. . . . Yet the girl seems nice—they both believe they will love each other for all eternity—may God bless them! I could do nothing but remonstrate [protest] and finally gave them my consent." Ferdinand and Antonie went on to have seven children before Ferdinand's death in 1891.

By 1874 Clara's arm pain caused her to turn down an invitation to attend the music festival in Cologne, Germany. Around the same time she was invited to perform in the United States, but decided not to go because of her arm. When the pain became unbearable, in January 1875 she went with Marie to a nursing home in Kiel and began an unusual rehabilitation. She noted in her diary that it was "a cure consisting in massage—which was very painful at first, but ceased to hurt after a few weeks." At first, she wrote, she played the piano for an hour each day despite the pain. After a while, the pain lessened, and Clara was able to return home to Berlin at the end of March.

But within a year the intense pain had returned. While in London, she was forced to give fewer concerts than she had anticipated. In between performances she rested her arm. Friends offered to help Clara financially, but she refused. She felt that she was still able to support her family.

In May she visited Ludwig at Colditz. He'd been asking his mother to come and take him home, and he did so again during her visit. She confided to her diary, "What agony to have to tell him that this could not be. It was all too awful for me! To see my child . . . virtually a prisoner. . . . His imploring eyes when I left—I shall never forget them!"

In June Clara returned to the nursing home in Kiel for another round of rehabilitation for her aching arm. Her life was about to change again. Pain in the arm of a concert pianist often meant the end of a career. Would she have to give up playing the piano?

Clara Schumann in her later years
(Courtesy of Mary Evans Picture Library/Alamy)

CHAPTER 10

Editor and Teacher

Clara's family troubles and the chronic arm
pain continued into 1877, yet she continued performing. She and Marie completed a concert tour
to Holland in the spring before returning to Berlin.

There, Brahms sent Clara more of his new music.
Clara played the pieces, analyzed them, and offered
musical comments. Occasionally, friends visited Clara
at home and played music with her. By July, she was
back in Baden-Baden again. Brahms sent her Bach's
Chaconne to be played on the piano with the left hand.
Clara was especially delighted with the piece because she
had strained a ligament in her right hand while opening
a drawer in her house. Now she had music she could play
and still give her right hand the rest it needed.

That summer she received more upsetting news. Word
came from her son-in-law Vittorio Marmorito that his and
Julie's eldest son had died. Clara was heartbroken, for that
grandson had always reminded her of Julie. All of the news
wasn't sad. In July, Clara learned that her daughter Elise
had become engaged to an American, Louis Sommerhoff.

The wedding would take place in November. Unlike her reactions to the engagements of Julie and Ferdinand, Clara seemed happy for Elise. Elise Schumann and Louis Sommerhoff were married on November 27, 1877.

In the meantime, Clara sent Brahms two of Felix's poems for comment. "Tell me, dear Johannes, what you think. Felix wants to print them, and this makes me anxious . . . ," Clara wrote to her friend. She feared that, because Felix was Robert Schumann's son, his poems might not be good enough to bear the Schumann name. Brahms agreed that Felix had some talent, but he was not altogether happy with the poems.

The weather turned cold as Clara arranged her next concert schedule. The weather worsened the pain in her arm so much that she turned down an invitation to perform in Frankfurt. But she stayed longer in Baden-Baden to address Felix's worsening health. Clara contacted his doctor about sending Felix to a place where the air would be better for him.

The doctor agreed and recommended Italy. In early October Clara sent her son to Sicily, and then left Baden-Baden to resume touring. By early 1878 she was thinking about moving to central Germany to reduce the strain of her concert travels. At the same time she received an offer to teach at a new Frankfurt music school, the Hoch Conservatory. With urging from Brahms, Clara accepted the job and moved to Frankfurt.

Clara's school contract required her to give nine lessons a week for eight months each year. She got her wish to have summer off and could take additional time off during the school year for short concert tours. By spring Clara found a house at Number 32 *Myliusstrasse* (Mylius Street) in Frankfurt. She packed her belongings and said goodbye to her friends in Berlin. Once in Frankfurt, she found time and energy in early 1878 to edit two of Robert's piano works—*Carnaval* and *Fantasiestucke*—for publication by Breitkopf & Hartel.

No sooner had Clara arrived in Frankfurt than she was off at once on a concert tour to Munich and other cities. In fact, it was October before she slept in her new home.

There, she found more worries about her children. Felix had returned from his unsuccessful health trip to Sicily, so Clara determined to try a tuberculosis treatment hospital in Falkenstein. Clara sent Eugenie, her youngest daughter, to stay with Felix at the hospital, about an hour from Frankfurt.

Clara worried to her friend Hermann Levi, "Felix has been in bed for the last 10 days; he will not let Eugenie leave him for a moment. She looks after him with a self-devotion which at once touches me and makes me anxious."

The hall yard in Frankfurt, Germany, around 1900

She confided to Brahms, "my heart is dejected . . . . To be old but healthy myself, and to see a son fade away in the flower of his years, this surely is one of the cruelest trials for a mother's heart."

The depressing family news contrasted sharply with the public adulation Clara was soon to receive for her remarkable half-century of musical work. October 20, 1878, marked the fiftieth anniversary of nine-year-old Clara's first public performance at the Leipzig *Gewandhaus*. A festival celebrating the occasion was held in Frankfurt at the Hoch Conservatory. In her diary, Clara called it "a day I shall never forget." She felt honored to be recognized by the musical community for a lifetime of devotion to music as a performer, editor, and composer.

That memorable day, the teachers played all of the music Clara had composed, most of it from earlier in her professional career. Clara had begun composing as a child

The *Gewandhaus* in Leipzig, Germany

and continued throughout her marriage. But when Robert died, she stopped composing in order to concentrate on performing to take care of her family financially.

After the celebration, Clara was greeted at home with gifts from the school, her friends from Frankfurt, and her children.

Clara described the most cherished gift, from her children and sons-in-law, as "a beautifully wrought slate clock, exquisitely painted after Raphael [a sixteenth century artist] and with all the children's names and some charming verses of Felix's engraved under the dial." As she read Felix's verses, she realized how much she loved and missed her son.

A second celebration of Clara's fiftieth year as a performer was held in Leipzig a few days later. A committee from the Leipzig *Gewandhaus* hosted Clara for the occasion. Clara wrote in her diary, "As I entered [the hall], the whole audience stood and a rain of flowers began, under which I was literally buried. . . . It was a long time before I could seat myself at the piano."

When she finished playing and responding to the applause, Clara was presented with a gold wreath. Each leaf on the wreath had the name of a composer whose music she had played during her career.

In November Felix and Eugenie came to Frankfurt to spend Christmas with Clara. It was the first time in many years that Felix was home, and Clara's heart ached when she saw her son. She wrote, "Ah! What a home-coming for our poor Felix! I thought him looking very ill, but he seemed in excellent spirits at seeing us again." She was sad to see Felix get weaker each day, but Clara worked hard not to let him see how worried she was. She wondered whether Felix suspected that this would be his last Christmas.

As Felix lingered in early 1879, Clara worried whenever she had to fulfill a concert obligation. Only her fierce discipline allowed her to perform. She later wrote, "Had I known how near was the end of our sufferer, I wouldn't have done it. My heart bled when I said good-night to Felix before going to the concert. . . . Yet I played with success, not missing a single note!"

Felix Schumann died on February 16, with Marie at his side. Clara's diary reads, "He suffered frightfully, a death-struggle in the fullest sense of the words. . . . I must confess I felt that it was a release for which I must thank heaven." She sent the news to Brahms in Vienna, but he was unable to go and comfort Clara.

Later, Clara told Hermann Levi that, "not only am I weighed down by grief for him whom I have lost, but I am also anxious and troubled about those whom I still possess." For the sake of her children who were still living, she wrote, she could not allow herself to sink into depression about Felix's death. She would set an example that would help them go on with their lives.

Clara's work, she said, was a great help in dealing with depression. She taught at the Conservatory and gave private lessons as well. Her days began with a half-hour walk before breakfast and another one after her lessons. She went shopping, visited friends, taught more lessons, and then returned home to receive visiting friends. When she had time, she continued to edit Robert's music for publication.

Clara had been the only woman on the faculty of the Hoch Conservatory when she began to teach there. When another woman applied in 1879, the director of the school turned down her application, confessing, "With the exception of Madame

A page from Brahms's piano concerto manuscript

Schumann there is no woman and there will not be any women employed in the Conservatory. As for Madame Schumann, I count her as a man." Clara had been hired in part because she was an accomplished musician and also because her fame throughout Europe would assure that students would enroll in the school.

But by October 1879 Clara was experiencing great pain in both arms. Brahms had sent her his concerto. Although Clara wanted to include it in her concerts that winter, playing the music strained her arms too much. Regretfully, she was forced to put the concerto aside.

Clara spent the following months exchanging visits and playing music with friends, including Joachim. At the same time, a writer named Max Kalbeck got Clara's permission to write a biography of Robert Schumann.

She continued to teach and to work on an edition of Robert's music that she had begun the previous year. Auditioning potential new students drained her of energy. She told Brahms, "almost every day some hopeful mother or father brings me their daughter to be tried, a thing which exhausts me mentally as well as physically since I have to send most of them away, and that always means tears."

As she assisted Kalbeck in preparing his manuscript, Clara reread letters she and Robert had written and experienced a new wave of grief. In August 1880 she wrote, "it makes me unspeakably sad for as I read these letters my heart once more throbs with passionate love for Him, the noblest and grandest of men, and I feel bitterly conscious of my loss." She recalled their struggles before and during their marriage. It was unfair, she thought, for people who loved each other as much as they did to have so little time together. Composing herself, she began to edit the letters, selecting ones that reflected the view of Robert she wanted the public to see.

The years that followed saw Clara giving fewer concerts than she had in the past. She did make a happy return to London in 1881 to give concerts and accept honorary membership in the prestigious Royal Academy of Music. Adding to the merriment, her daughter Elise and her husband and children arrived from America to visit Clara in London.

But the pain in her arm was now so intense that she was often unable to play the piano. She still enjoyed music-filled Christmases at home in Berlin with family, friends, and even some of her students. Brahms was often there, bringing his latest musical compositions.

She continued to experience the emotional ups and downs of editing Robert's letters. Late in 1884 she wrote in her diary, "These letters awaken my longing more than words can say, and my heart's wounds bleed afresh. What have I possessed and lost!" She wondered how she found the strength to go on living without Robert, but realized that her art and her love for her children sustained her.

By May 1885 she had finished editing the letters. She wrote, "We finished the letters. We decided to publish only Robert's early letters to his mother, to me and to a few friends." She excluded the letters Robert had written to her during the time he and Clara had been engaged, because she thought they were too personal.

That fall, although saddened by the death of her brother Alwin at age sixty-four, Clara continued an active schedule. She performed at a new concert hall in the Leipzig *Gewandhaus* and found the acoustics were wonderful. She happily examined in minute detail music Brahms had sent her for his fourth symphony.

But now, Clara's hearing began to deteriorate. In February 1886, after attending a rehearsal for Robert's concerto, she admitted, "My hearing is now so bad that I cannot follow any music properly, it is all blurred, and often I hear all the higher parts a semi-tone too high."

Fortunately, her hearing problem would have little effect on her next big project: Breitkopf & Hartel would publish a second volume of Robert's letters, including letters to Brahms, Joachim, Felix Mendelssohn, and others. Clara also found time to work on another edition of Robert's piano music, adding suggestions on how to play the music. Ever the perfectionist, Clara wrote, "It is clear to me that I must do it, so that at least one correct edition will be available for students."

CHAPTER 11

The Last Years

After Clara Schumann finished editing Robert's letters and annotating the *Instructive Edition* of his piano music, in March 1887 she returned to London. This time, she played Robert's piano pieces for the daughters of the Princess of Wales. As a gift, the Princess of Wales gave Clara a jeweled swan holding a lyre (a small musical instrument in the harp family). Clara returned to Frankfurt in April for a short while. At the end of the month, she and Marie had an audience with the Princess of Prussia, which Clara had requested. Clara noted her purpose in her diary, "She [the Princess] had recently founded 5 scholarships at the *Louisenstift* [a girls' school in Berlin] and I hoped to obtain one of these for Julie [Clara's granddaughter, Ferdinand's daughter]."

Although the princess was polite, asked questions about her granddaughter, and took notes when Clara answered, there were no scholarships available. All of them had long ago been promised to other students. Clara was disappointed. Although she was the most famous concert pianist in all of

Europe and worked steadily, there was not enough money to send her granddaughter to *Louisenstift*.

During February of the following year, Clara went to London again to perform. But now she found that playing the piano at a concert level exhausted her energy. She did not take the same pleasure in performing that she had in the past. Also, most of her London friends were either ill or too old to enjoy life in the way they had in the past. Clara decided that this would be her last concert tour in London. In March she wrote in her diary, "it is my decision that the England journeys must now end, which grieves me beyond measure. How hard it is to stop voluntarily, when one could still go on! But this resolution is surely right, as my health just won't resist the strain much longer."

In the spring, Clara welcomed a familiar visitor. "Emilie List, my oldest friend, came once more to pay me a fortnight's visit . . . we have so many common memories which go back almost to the days of childhood," she wrote. Their conversations and memories must have been fresh in Clara's mind as she embarked on a new tour of Germany with Marie and Eugenie. They all visited the Weimar home of Johann Wolfgang von Goethe, where nine-year-old Clara had once played the piano for the poet. His home was now a museum, and

German poet and philosopher Wolfgang von Goethe

the piano she had played was still in the house. "It affected me strangely," she wrote. "A whole life has been lived since then."

The women saw Ferdinand, who was under treatment for morphine addiction in Kostritz. Clara recorded the bittersweet visit: "We found Ferdinand . . . looking very well but getting about painfully on two sticks. . . . It is scarcely likely that he will ever be able to walk again. . . . We left for Schneeberg [another stop on the tour] with heavy hearts."

Clara and her daughters returned home in time to celebrate Clara's "diamond jubilee," commemorating her sixtieth year as a concert artist. She described the celebration to Rosalie Leser: "Everyone [in the audience] stood up when I appeared, there was a flourish of trumpets, and endless cheering and applauding."

"I never suspected how much love was bestowed on me, and I am often quite embarrassed," she wrote after receiving letters, telegrams, and flowers from admirers around the world.

Despite her poor health, Clara continued to perform into January 1898. She also continued to teach students who came to her from all over Germany, other parts of Europe, and the United States. Because she was a world-renowned concert artist, students clamored to study with her. One student from England was overjoyed when he was chosen as one of Clara's students. "I am proud to be a Schumann scholar now," he wrote. "I would never have dreamed how difficult it would be to be accepted in her class. Everyone in my generation is trying for it." To handle the demand, Clara focused on students who were musically advanced, while Marie and Eugenie taught the less-advanced ones.

On September 13, 1889, Clara celebrated her seventieth birthday at the retreat home in Baden-Baden. She had mixed feelings about the milestone, noting, "It has come at last—the seventieth—ought I to rejoice? It is at best but a melancholy joy. Much love still surrounds me, but yet how many do we miss!" The occasion, arranged by Marie and Eugenie, was a remarkable convergence of great music: Joachim played Robert's *Phantasie* for her, and Brahms brought a new piece of his music, which Clara would later play when she returned to Frankfurt.

At one of the birthday parties, Clara realized that she was surrounded both by people who loved her and by the memories of many others she had lost. "At bedtime I had only one desire, one thought: that Heaven might allow me to enjoy the love of my children a few years longer, not in infirmity, but with the vigor that still stirs in my heart," she wrote in her diary after the birthday celebration.

Back in Frankfurt, Clara delighted in the music Brahms had given her but found it physically agonizing to play. She wrote in her diary,

> *I am currently reveling in Brahms's Third Sonata, which I have started practicing for our quartet. To my vast sorrow it is a great strain for me to play. . . . Ah, how am I ever to live on, if I should have to give it up altogether?*

Johannes Brahms in his later years

The pain made her nervous about accepting a recital invitation from the Frankfurt Museum. And although it went well, when the recital ended, Clara decided it would be one of her last performances. It was just as well, for her hearing loss was now quite severe. When Brahms accompanied her to the theater, Clara could not hear a good part of the dialogue. Later she attended a concert but heard little of the music.

By early 1890 doctors believed Ferdinand Schumann was cured of his dependency on morphine and ready to return home to his wife and family. But he relapsed and began to take drugs again. Ferdinand died on June 6. Unable to attend the funeral, Clara wrote, "I am deeply saddened, yet I must say it was a deliverance for the poor boy. What dreary years he has lived through." Of her eight children, four were still alive: Ludwig, who still suffered mental problems, and three daughters, Marie, Elise, and Eugenie.

On March 13, 1891, Clara gave her final public performance in Frankfurt. It was clearly for the best: by this time her hearing problems and the pain in her arms were so severe that she could barely perform. But it was becoming clearer that her own body of musical work would endure. Breitkopf & Hartel asked to publish the cadenzas that Clara had written and played in her concerts. Cadenzas are solo passages within a larger musical work, usually a concerto. Clara was eager to have them published, but worried that one of them contained a small amount of music that Brahms had written. She wrote to him in Vienna for his permission and to ask whether he wanted to be credited as co-composer.

Brahms wrote back to his friend, "I beg you with all my heart to let the cadenza be printed over your name."

The cadenza, he insisted, was hers and he had only contributed a small amount.

Despite the happy publishing news, life now became more difficult. In January 1892 Clara fell and sprained her right arm. The next month she contracted a lung infection and was forced to give up her teaching position at the Conservatory. Fortunately, Marie and Eugenie were on hand to nurse their mother back to health. Eugenie covered Clara's piano lessons during the day and cared for her mother at night. The effort strained Eugenie's own health, too. She was diagnosed with tuberculosis but recovered enough by April to resume piano lessons.

That summer Clara and Marie traveled to Interlaken, Switzerland. Their hotel window looked out over a mountain garden where Clara took walks. There, the two would often "visit the old Church with its ruined grave-yard, and at last in the village—a fascinating village with nearly all the houses built by wood-carvers—find my bath-chair, in which I would return, while Marie walked." The lake breezes and beautiful sunsets over the lake seemed to rejuvenate Clara.

In October Eugenie took a job as a piano teacher in England, where she would live the rest of her life. Her recitals were well received by English audiences, who must have recalled her mother's remarkable concerts. Although Eugenie returned to Frankfurt each year to visit, Clara felt the loss of close contact deeply. She wrote in her diary, "Bad nights, filled with gloomy broodings. I am so defeated, it hurts. My life is finished, with nothing more to look forward to, yet when a heart remains as sturdy as mine this is hard to bear."

Clara was now seventy-three, and had only Marie at home with her. Marie wrote and answered letters for her mother and was at her mother's side when visitors came to the house. She also attended concerts for Clara and brought back accounts of how they went.

Christmastime brought a beloved visitor: Brahms arrived with new works, which Clara was able to play on the piano in her music room. But she often dwelled on the loss of her career as a concert artist. She wrote, "How often the thought besets me nowadays that I shall be forgotten even while still alive! That's the way it is with interpretive artists; once they leave the footlights they are remembered by no one save perhaps their contemporaries." Clara believed that the younger generation wouldn't know her name and would only smile indulgently when someone mentioned it.

It was even more difficult for her to play the piano now because of the pain in her arms and the problems with her hearing. She wrote in February 1894, "What will become of me if I cannot play any more?"

Although she had given up her position at the Conservatory, she still had a few students, including Ferdinand's son. Clara had tried to dissuade him from becoming a musician, but relented after he pleaded with her.

In 1894 and 1895, Clara returned to Interlaken for summer vacations, although the lakeside retreat was her second choice. She had wanted to visit Paris, but the city and its society were embroiled in military and political scandals including the trial of Alfred Dreyfus. Dreyfus, a captain in the French army, was falsely accused of giving classified information to the German government. The political unrest that resulted convinced Clara that Switzerland would be a better vacation choice.

But the quiet inactivity of Interlaken depressed Clara. Her diary says, "How long are the days without work! And even

Clara Schumann circa 1888
(Courtesy of Mary Evans Picture Library/Alamy)

if I try working, what can I do that will not hurt my eyes or my back?" She could no longer read for any length of time, write, or play the piano. She felt that she was a burden to Marie, who now cared for her as if for a child. By the following year, travel became a great hardship for Clara. She lost her appetite and ate very little. As a result she lost weight and looked haggard. "My evenings are dreadful. I am so faint that I can hardly sit up, and something is terribly wrong with my stomach. . . . I feel as if I were dying. Poor Marie nurses me day and night—oh!—and weeps with me when I am depressed," her diary notes.

By March 1896 Clara spent a great deal of time at home in her bed. Marie took her mother on carriage rides on sunny days when possible. But on one such outing, Marie noticed that Clara's face was ashen and they quickly returned home. While the color returned to Clara's face, Marie noticed a change in her mother's ability to speak. Clara slurred her words. When she signed an autograph for a young admirer, her handwriting resembled a series of scratches. A doctor diagnosed a slight stroke, a clot in the brain that stops the flow of blood and may cause cells in that part of the brain to die.

Marie broke the news by letter to Brahms in Vienna. Brahms replied, "with a heavy heart I must ask you, if you think the worst is to be expected, to be so good as to let me know, so that I may come while those dear eyes are still open; for when they close so much will end for me!"

It would not be long. When Clara's health worsened, Marie sent Brahms an urgent telegram. He traveled to Frankfurt quickly but arrived too late to talk with his old friend. Clara Schumann died on May 10, 1896. Brahms accompanied her body to Bonn, where she was buried beside her beloved Robert.

After the funeral, Brahms returned to Vienna, but it seemed he had lost his own will to live, too. His own health deteriorated, and he gave his last concert on March 7, 1897, and died on April 3, 1898.

Clara Schumann, "The Queen of the Piano," was applauded by audiences and showered with flowers, honors, and jewels during a career of six decades. But unlike other musical giants of her time, she also was dealing with many of the challenges of today's women, juggling career, marriage, and family responsibilities. And, contrary to her fear that younger generations would not know her name, Clara Schumann's appeal has endured. Her body of musical work remains popular, and she even enjoys a posthumous profile on the social networking site Facebook. Though known as a piano virtuoso of the Romantic era, Clara Schumann has proven that she is a woman for all time.

CLARA SCHUMANN

Timeline

1819	Born in Leipzig, Germany, on September 13; second of five children of Friedrich Wieck and Marianne Tromlitz.
1824	Begins to take piano lessons from father.
1825	Parents divorce; mother marries Adolph Bargiel and moves to Berlin in 1826.
1828	Gives first public performance at Leipzig *Gewandhaus*.
1830	Composes first piano compositions; shares her childhood home with Robert Schumann, who moves in to the Wieck house to study piano.
1831	Composes another group of piano pieces; makes first concert tour with father.
1834	Builds reputation in Europe as child prodigy; continues to compose and tour.
1835	Falls in love with Robert Schumann; father determined to keep them apart.

1837	Becomes secretly engaged to Robert Schumann.
1839	Petitions court in Leipzig to allow marriage to Robert because her father refuses consent.
1840	Marries Robert Schumann on September 12.
1841	Daughter Marie born on September 1.
1843	Daughter Elise born on April 25; reconciles with father.
1844	Travels with husband to give concerts in Russia; Robert begins to have bouts of depression.
1845	Daughter Julie born on March 11; composes Trio in G Minor for violin, cello, and piano.
1846	Son Emil born on February 8.

(continued on next page)

1847	Emil dies on June 22.
1848	Son Ludwig born on January 20.
1849	Son Ferdinand born on July 16.
1851	Daughter Eugenie born on December 1.
1853	Begins friendship, along with husband Robert, with composer Johannes Brahms.
1854	Husband hospitalized with mental illness; son Felix born on June 11.
1856	Robert Schumann dies on July 29.
1857	Begins to have pains in left arm, forcing concert cancellations.
1858-1867	Continues to tour despite increasing arm pain; spends Christmas and summer holidays with her children.
1869	Daughter Julie marries on September 22.
1870	Son Ludwig hospitalized with mental illness; son Ferdinand is drafted into army.
1871	Son Ferdinand returns home addicted to morphine.
1872	Daughter Julie dies on November 10; mother Marianne Tromlitz dies on March 10
1873	Father Frederick Wieck dies on October 6; son Ferdinand marries.

1876–1877	Pain in arm becomes more intense; despite pain, continues to travel and perform.
1877	Daughter Elise marries on November 27.
1878	Begins teaching piano to advanced students at Hoch Conservatory; celebrates fiftieth anniversary as concert performer on October 20.
1879	Son Felix dies on February 16; pain spreads to right arm.
1879–1885	Continues to edit husband's music and letters for publication; gives fewer concerts.
1888	Celebrates sixtieth anniversary as concert performer.
1891	Son Ferdinand dies on June 6; gives final public performance and retires from concert stage.
1896	Suffers slight stroke; dies on May 20.

Sources

Chapter One: Waiting for Something to Say

p. 14,   "skill, confidence, and diligence," Jane Bowers and Judith Tick, eds. *Women Making Music: The Western Art Tradition, 1150-1950* (Urbana, IL: University of Illinois Press, 1986), 253.

p. 16,   "My Diary . . ." Ibid., 254.

p. 16,   "On September 18th . . ." Berthold Litzmann, *Clara Schumann: An Artist's Life Based on Material Found in Diaries and Letters, Vol. 1* (New York: Vienna House, 1972), 3.

p. 16,   "I heard a grand symphony . . ." Ibid., 5.

p. 17,   "My daughters . . ." Nancy B. Reich, *Clara Schumann: The Artist and the Woman* (Ithaca, New York: Cornell University Press, 1985), 44.

p. 17,   "my perception of music . . ." Litzmann, *Clara Schumann: An Artist's Life,* 6.

p. 18,   "Everything went quite well . . ." Bertita Harding, *Concerto: The Glowing Story of Clara Schumann* (Indianapolis, Indiana: The Bobbs-Merrill Company, Inc., 1961), 16.

p. 18,   "I made fewer mistakes . . ." Litzmann, *Clara Schumann: An Artist's Life,* 10.

p. 20,   "It went very well . . ." Ibid., 11.

p. 20,   "I quite forgot . . ." Ibid., 13.

Chapter Two: Child Prodigy

p. 21,   "The sensation the two apes . . ." Reich, *Clara Schumann: The Artist*, 47.

p. 23,   "Chopin's Variations . . ." Litzmann, *Clara Schumann: An Artist's Life*, 23.

p. 24,   "and played charades . . ." Reich, *Clara Schumann: The Artist*, 62.

p. 24, "This young artist's . . ." Janet Nichols, *Women Music Makers: An Introduction to Women Composers* (New York: Walker & Company, 1992), 37.

p. 26, "We found him reading . . ." Litzmann, *Clara Schumann: An Artist's Life*, 25.

p. 26, "admired Clara's intelligent . . ." Ibid., 25.

p. 26, "In the first place . . ." Ibid., 34.

p. 26-27, "I have been in Arabia . . ." Ibid.

p. 28, "Even in her first piece . . ." Reich, *Clara Schumann: The Artist,* 48.

p. 29, "Clara arrived early yesterday . . ." Bowers and Tick, *Women Making Music*, 257.

p. 29, "Clara is prettier and taller . . ." Ibid., 257.

p. 29, "Clara is stubborn . . ." Harding, *Concerto*, 34.

p. 32, "When you gave me . . ." Reich, *Clara Schumann: The Artist,* 70.

Chapter Three: The Secret Engagement

p. 37, "What a letter of recommendation . . ." Reich, *Clara Schumann: The Artist* , 79-80.

p. 38, "I am very upset . . ." Ibid., 82.

p. 38, "You are, forgive me . . ." Ibid., 88.

p. 39, "since you value my ring . . ." Carol Neuls-Bates, ed., *Women in Music: An Anthology of Source Readings from the Middle Ages to the Present* (New York: Harper & Row, Publishers, 1982), 97.

p. 39, "How much one has to do . . ." Ibid., 92.

p. 39, "I talked to Father . . ." Litzmann, *Clara Schumann: An Artist's Life*, 137-138.

p. 40, "I can give a concert . . ." Ibid., 138.

p. 40, "For your sake . . ." Reich, *Clara Schumann: The Artist,* 88.

p. 44, "I could not look at my father . . ." Ronald Taylor, *Robert Schumann: His Life and Work* (New York: Universe Books, 1982), 177.

Chapter Four: The Early Years of Marriage

p. 47,   "This book . . ." Harding, *Concerto*, 83.

p. 47,   "We have been married . . ." Reich, *Clara Schumann: The Artist*, 104.

p. 48,   "I was received . . ." Ibid., 110.

p. 51,   "I wanted to write . . ." Ibid., 115.

p. 53,   "that I'd left you . . ." Ibid., 114.

p. 53,   "I earn nothing at home . . ." Neuls-Bates, *Women in Music*, 98.

p. 54,   "Am I to neglect . . ." Ibid., 98.

p. 54,   "If only the room . . ." Harding, *Concerto,* 89.

p. 54,   "I am getting behind . . ." Taylor, *Robert Schumann*, 186.

p. 55,   "I should have been . . ." Litzmann, *Clara Schumann: An Artist's Life,* 309.

p. 55,   "Father is now heart and soul . . ." Reich, *Clara Schumann: The Artist,* 106.

p. 56,   "There is a strange silence . . ." Ibid., 117.

p. 59,   "Schumann was . . ." Ibid., 120-121.

p. 60,   "Robert didn't sleep . . ." Ibid., 122.

Chapter Five: A Time of Strife

p. 61,   "great pleasure . . ." Litzmann, *Clara Schumann: An Artist's Life*, 402.

p. 62,   "effeminate and sentimental . . ." Nichols, *Women Music Makers*, 52.

p. 62,   "Robert has added . . ." Litzmann, *Clara Schumann: An Artist's Life,* 404.

p. 62,   "She lacks spirit . . ." Harding, *Concerto*, 97.

p. 65,   "he forced me to play it . . ." Litzmann, *Clara Schumann: An Artist's Life,* 373.

p. 66,   "There is nothing greater . . ." Ibid., 410.

p. 66,   "I shall never . . ." Ibid., 421.

p. 67,   "It was so pleasant . . ." Ibid., 431.

p. 68,   "I have taken . . ." Ibid., 429.

p. 68,   "A woman must not wish . . ." *Composers: Clara Wieck Schumann*, http://www.essentialsofmusic.com/composer/ schumann_c.html.

p. 69,   "Happy as I was . . ." Litzmann, *Clara Schumann: An Artist's Life,* 431.

p. 70,   "And what will become . . ." Taylor, *Robert Schumann*, 249.

p. 70,   "But Robert says . . ." Litzmann, *Clara Schumann: An Artist's Life,* 398.

p. 71,   "My piano playing . . ." Nichols, *Women Music Makers*, 48.

p. 73,   "we live in a state . . ." Litzmann, *Clara Schumann: An Artist's Life,* 461.

Chapter Six: Dark Clouds Gather

p. 75,   "I absolutely can't get used . . ." Harding, *Concerto*, 112.

p. 76,   "Could this mean . . ." Ibid., 113.

p. 78,   "If I did not . . ." Nichols, *Women Music Makers*, 54.

p. 78,   "There is nothing . . ." Reich, *Clara Schumann: The Artist*, 136.

p. 80,   "One day— . . ." Walter Frisch, ed, *Brahms and His World* (Princeton, New Jersey: Princeton University Press, 1990), 41.

p. 80,   "It is really moving . . ." Joan Chissell, *The Great Composers: Brahms* (London, England: Faber & Faber, 1977), 23.

p. 82,   "What a shameful plot . . ." John Daverio, *Robert Schumann: Herald of a "New Poetic Age"* (New York: Oxford University Press, 1997), 456.

p. 82,   "With 6 children . . ." Harding, *Concerto,* 118.

p. 83-84, "Even as we were sitting . . ." Reich, *Clara Schumann: The Artist,* 142.

p. 85-86, "When I merely touched him . . ." Ibid., 143.

Chapter Seven: A Deepening Friendship

p. 87,   "Him, the magnificent . . ." Nichols, *Women Music Makers*, 55-56.

p. 88,   "It was a hard . . ." Litzmann, *Clara Schumann: An Artist's Life*, 60.

p. 88,   "That good Brahms . . ." Ibid., 69.

p. 88,   "I feel very unwell . . ." Ibid., 69.

p. 89,   "I feel paralyzed . . ." Harding, *Concerto*, 130.

p. 89,   "looking old . . ." Reich, *Clara Schumann: The Artist*, 147.

p. 91,   "I am haunted . . ." Ibid., 133.

p. 91-92, "Oh, if I could see . . ." Florence May, *The Life of Johannes Brahms, Vol. 1* (Neptune City, New Jersey: Paganiniana Publications, Inc., 1981), 175.

p. 92,   "I . . . believe that a quieter life . . ." Nichols, *Women Music Makers*, 58.

p. 94,   "It made me sad . . ." Litzmann, *Clara Schumann: An Artist's Life,* 93.

p. 95,   "A year ago to-day . . ." Ibid., 103.

p. 95-96, "He was very merry . . ." Ibid., 108.

p. 98,   "We three . . ." Ibid., 120.

Chapter Eight: Widowhood

p. 100, "I let my hands lie . . ." Litzmann, *Clara Schumann: An Artist's Life,* 134-135.

p. 100, "What a thought . . ." Reich, *Clara Schumann: The Artist,* 149-150.

p. 100, "For weeks he had had . . ." Ibid., 150.

p. 101, "I stood at the body . . ." Ibid., 151.

p. 101, "God give me strength . . ." Litzmann, *Clara Schumann: An Artist's Life,* 140.

p. 101, "I had come there . . ." Ibid., 152.

p. 102, "I felt terrible . . ." Reich, *Clara Schumann: The Artist,* 157.

p. 103-104, "Upon medical examination . . ." Litzmann, *Clara Schumann: An Artist's Life,* 153.

p. 104, "I ask nothing more for him . . ." Reich, *Clara Schumann: The Artist,* 157.

p. 105, "Just think . . ." Harding, *Concerto,* 152.

p. 105, "Wherever she might be . . ." Nichols, *Women Music Makers*, 58.

p. 105, "What do you say . . ." Litzmann, *Clara Schumann: An Artist's Life,* 179.

p. 107, "Schumann himself . . ." Ibid., 183.

p. 108, "On Christmas Eve . . ." Marie Busch, *Memoirs of Eugenie Schumann* (London: Eulenburg Books, 1985), 11.

p. 109, "I am so glad . . ." Litzmann, *Clara Schumann: An Artist's Life,* 208.

p. 110, "It has given me . . ." Ibid., 222.

Chapter Nine: Family Troubles

p. 111, "My heart bleeds . . ." Harding, *Concerto,* 185.

p. 112, "You can live . . ." Ibid., 176.

p. 113, "I have told her . . ." Ibid., 181.

p. 113,   "struck my heart . . ." Reich, *Clara Schumann: The Artist,* 164.

p. 113,   "I have not felt . . ." Ibid., 164.

p. 113,   "No-one is allowed . . ." Litzmann, *Clara Schumann: An Artist's Life,* 274.

p. 114-115, "Just think . . ." Harding, *Concerto,* 185.

p. 116,   "When it was all over . . ." Ibid., 193.

p. 118,   "I am calm . . ." Reich, *Clara Schumann: The Artist,* 163.

p. 118,   "I am deeply shaken . . ." Harding, *Concerto,* 200.

p. 119,   "now, with one stroke . . ." Reich, *Clara Schumann: The Artist,* 167.

p. 119,   "a cure consisting of . . ." Litzmann, *Clara Schumann: An Artist's Life,* 308.

p. 119,   "What agony . . ." Harding, *Concerto,* 202.

Chapter Ten: Editor and Teacher

p. 122,   "Tell me, dear Johannes . . ." Litzmann, *Clara Schumann: An Artist's Life*, 327.

p. 123,   "Felix has been . . ." Ibid., 341.

p. 124,   "my heart is dejected . . ." Harding, *Concerto*, 207.

p. 124,   "a day I shall never forget." Litzmann, *Clara Schumann: An Artist's Life,* 341.

p. 125,   "a beautifully . . ." Ibid., 342.

p. 125,   "As I entered . . ." Reich, *Clara Schumann: The Artist,* 181.

p. 125,   "Ah! What a home-coming . . ." Litzmann, *Clara Schumann: An Artist's Life,* 344.

p. 126,   "Had I known . . ." Harding, *Concerto,* 208-209.

p. 126,   "He suffered . . ." Litzmann, *Clara Schumann: An Artist's Life,* 346.

p. 126,   "not only am I weighed down . . ." Ibid., 347.

p. 126, 128, "With the exception . . ." Reich, *Clara Schumann: The Artist,* 292.

p. 128,   "almost every day . . ." Litzmann, *Clara Schumann: An Artist's Life,* 354.

p. 128,   "it makes me unspeakably sad . . ." Ibid., 355.

p. 129,   "These letters . . ." Ibid., 376.

p. 129,   "We finished the letters . . ." Ibid., 380.

p. 130,   "My hearing is now so bad . . ." Ibid., 383-384.
p. 130,   "It is clear to me . . ." Reich, *Clara Schumann: The Artist,* 255.

Chapter Eleven: The Last Years

p. 131,   "She had recently . . ." Litzmann, *Clara Schumann: An Artist's Life,* 389.
p. 132,   "it is my decision . . ." Harding, *Concerto,* 230.
p. 132,   "Emilie List . . ." Litzmann, *Clara Schumann: An Artist's Life,* 395.
p. 133,   "It affected me . . ." Ibid., 395.
p. 133,   "We found Ferdinand . . ." Ibid., 396.
p. 133,   "Everyone . . ." Ibid., 399.
p. 133,   "I never suspected . . ." Reich, *Clara Schumann: The Artist,* 181.
p. 133,   "I am proud to be . . ." Ibid., 293.
p. 133-134, "It has come at last . . ." Litzmann, *Clara Schumann: An Artist's Life,* 402-403.
p. 134,   "At bedtime . . ." Harding, *Concerto,* 236.
p. 134,   "I am currently . . ." Ibid., 237.
p. 136,   "I am deeply . . ." Ibid., 240.
p. 136,   "I beg you . . ." Ibid., 242.
p. 137,   "visit the old Church . . ." Litzmann, *Clara Schumann: An Artist's Life,* 415.
p. 137,   "Bad nights . . ." Harding, *Concerto,* 245.
p. 138,   "How often the thought . . ." Ibid., 246.
p. 138,   "What will become of me . . ." Reich, *Clara Schumann: The Artist,* 183.
p. 138, 140 "How long are the days . . ." Harding, *Concerto,* 250.
p. 140,   "My evenings are . . ." Ibid., 252.
p. 140,   "with a heavy heart . . ." Ivor Keys, *Johannes Brahms* (Portland, Oregon: Amadeus Press, 1989), 152.

Bibliography

Bowers, Jane, and Judith Tick, eds. *Women Making Music: The Western Art Tradition, 1150-1950*. Urbana, IL: University of Illinois Press, 1986.

Busch, Marie, trans. *Memoirs of Eugenie Schumann*. London: Ernst Eulenburg Ltd., 1985.

Chissell, Joan. *The Great Composers: Brahms*. London: Faber & Faber, 1977.

Cohen, Aaron I. *International Encyclopedia of Women Composers, Vol. 2*. New York: Books and Music (USA) Inc., 1987.

Composers: Clara Wieck Schumann, http://www.essentialsofmusic.com/composer/schumann_c.html.

Daverio, John. *Robert Schumann: Herald of a "New Poetic Age."* New York: Oxford University Press, 1997.

————. *Crossing Paths: Schubert, Schumann, and Brahms*. New York: Oxford University Press, 2002.

Dickinson, June M., compiler. *Reminiscences of Clara Schumann from the Diary of Her Granson Ferdinand Schumann*. New York: Musical Scope Publishers, 1973.

Fanny Mendelssohn, Clara Schumann: Piano Trio/Dartington, CD-ROM. London: Hyperion, 1988.

Frisch, Walter, ed. *Brahms and His World*. Princeton, New Jersey: Princeton University Press, 1990.

Glickman, Sylvia, and Martha Furman Schleifer, eds. *Women Composers & Music Through the Years, Vol. 6*. New York: G. K. Hall & Co., 1999.

Harding, Bertita. *Concerto: The Glowing Story of Clara Schumann*. Indianapolis, Indiana: The Bobbs-Merrill Company, Inc., 1961.

Jensen, Eric Frederick. *Schumann*. London, England: Oxford University Press, 2001.

Jezic, Diane Peacock. *Women Composers: The Lost Tradition Found*. New York: The Feminist Press, 1988

Keys, Ivor. *Johannes Brahms*. Portland, Oregon: Amadeus Press, 1989.

Litzmann, Berthold. *Clara Schumann: An Artist's Life Based on Material Found in Diaries and Letters, Vols.1 & 2*. New York: Vienna House, 1972.

May, Florence. *The Life of Johannes Brahms, Vols. 1& 2*. Neptune City, New Jersey: Paganiniana Publications, Inc., 1981.

Neuls-Bates, Carol, ed. *Women in Music: An Anthology f Source Readings from the Middle Ages to the Present*. New York: Harper & Row, Publishers, 1982.

Nichols, Janet. *Women Music Makers: An Introduction to Women Composers*. New York: Walker & Company, 1992.

Norderval, Kristin. "Clara Schumann and her Songs," http://www.norderval.org/Schumann.htm.

Reich, Nancy B. *Clara Schumann: The Artist and the Woman*. Ithaca, New York: Cornell University Press, 1985.

Sadie, Julie Anne, and Rhian Samuel, eds. *The New Grove Dictionary of Women Composers*. London: Macmillan, Ltd., 1994.

Schonberg, Harold C. *The Great Pianists*. New York: Simon and Schuster, 1968.

Taylor, Ronald. *Robert Schumann: His Life and Work*. New York: Universe Books, 1982.

The Women's Philharmonic: Lili Boulanger, Clara Schumann, Germaine Tailleferre, Fanny Mendelssohn. CD-ROM. Westbury, N.Y.: Koch International Classics, 1992.

Web sites

http://www.scils.rutgers.edu/~eversr/biogral.html
This Rutgers University site contains information about Clara Schumann, including samples of her compositions, a comprehensive listing of both existing and lost compositions, photographs, a bibliography, and an extensive timeline.

http://geneva.edu/~dksmith/clara/worklst.html
A listing (in German) by genre of the songs, piano music, and orchestral music Clara Schumann wrote, along with the years when they were created and/or published.

http://www.geneva.edu/~dksmith/clara/lyric2.html#walzer
This Web site contains translations of songs Clara Schumann wrote.

Book cover and interior design by Derrick Carroll.

Index